MORE FROM LESS

YOMI MAKANJUOLA

MORE FROM LESS

© Yomi Makanjuola
First published in December 2020
9yoma9@gmail.com

All rights reserved, including the right to reproduce this book or portions thereof in any form whatsoever.

PREFACE

I don't know about you, but sometimes when using the Google search engine, I chuckle at the peripheral deadbeat *I'm Feeling Lucky* button, which is almost redundant. To my mind, *I'm Feeling Lucky* serves as a metaphor for information overload and material excess, especially for people in affluent nations who are highly susceptible to attention deficit and decision fatigue. That said, for those who were *lucky* enough to come of age in a hyperactive, social media-obsessed consumer culture, the idea of too much of anything might seem quaint. Furthermore, concepts such as frugality, minimalism and simplicity could sound outright bizarre.

Paradoxically, this same millennial generation that could hardly lay claim to a conservation ethos is engaged in the fight to save the environment and possibly reverse climate change meltdown. To mitigate this existential threat, it seems to me that we all need to take a deep breath, stop pointing fingers at each other, and settle down to agree what shape we wish to bequeath our planet to future generations. As the world edges towards the precipice of colossal self-harm, it would be unhelpful to overstate the challenge, but equally it would be reckless to ignore it altogether.

The basic underpinning of *More from Less* is that the quantum of most resources is finite; therefore, in a competitive marketplace, this should encourage strategies for loss reduction, cost savings, streamlined processes, simpler operations, and the innovative use of technology for sustainable growth. By the same logic, if the aggregate quantity of a resource is perceived to be infinite and unregulated, consumption might have no bounds.

During my years at Accenture, I specialised in the process and technology skill domains where the rule of thumb implied that good technology cannot mask a poorly defined business process. As a systems integrator, the constant challenge was how to optimise the alignment of people, processes and technology to achieve superior performance and efficiency gains in a globalised business landscape. Implicitly, I discovered that simplicity trumps complexity while a minimalist mindset is hard to instil.

To that end, any organisation that is able to offer differentiated products and services fastest at the right price, while delivering high quality and exceptional customer service, trounces the competition. However, building a corporate culture with a winning mentality needs strong leadership with a clear vision. It also requires developing the management skills to execute a corporate strategy that drives creative investments and the judicious allocation of resources for the best outcomes.

To be sure, the scope of this book extends beyond the corporate world to grimy industrial production, waste management, energy, and the environment, down to how the idea of *More from Less* can help you live an imaginative, prudent and enriched life that benefits your family, organisation, community and, dare I say, the world at large. In the spirit of good stewardship, are we all ready to heed the call to consume less and conserve more?

CONTENTS

Chapter 1: *Time's Always Running Away*   1

Chapter 2: *Hardly Simple*   5

Chapter 3: *Energy Blues*   9

Chapter 4: *Ma Lessons*   14

Chapter 5: *The Coming Revolution*   18

Chapter 6: *Parched Parched Parched*   23

Chapter 7: *Law and Othèr*   27

Chapter 8: *Zero-Sum Delusion*   31

Chapter 9: *Déjà Vu?*   35

Chapter 10: *Joe & Jo Pleb*   40

Chapter 11: *Jack Ma's Catch-22*   44

Chapter 12:	*Building Blocks*	49
Chapter 13:	*Visually Speaking*	54
Chapter 14:	*Poor Earth*	59
Chapter 15:	*Alternative Intelligence*	64
Chapter 16:	*Squeezed*	69
Chapter 17:	*Trust Me*	74
Chapter 18:	*Cat On A Hot Tin Roof*	79
Chapter 19:	*Social Division*	84
Chapter 20:	*Waterloo*	90
Chapter 21:	*Reform, Not*	96
Chapter 22:	*Hand-Me-Down*	102
Chapter 23:	*Plastics Everywhere*	108

Chapter 24:	*Crossroads*	114
Chapter 25:	*Out of Sight*	118
Chapter 26:	*Tainted Glass*	123
Chapter 27:	*Cuckoo's Nest*	129
Chapter 28:	*S.T.E.A.M.*	135
Chapter 29:	*Elementary*	142
Chapter 30:	*Play On*	148
Chapter 31:	*Hubris*	154
Chapter 32:	*Crestfallen*	160
Chapter 33:	*Antsy*	165
Chapter 34:	*Gumption*	171

Chapter 35:	*Startup On A Pittance*	177
Chapter 36:	*Timeout On Dirty Energy*	186
Chapter 37:	*Erosion of Middle-Class Jobs*	195
Chapter 38:	*Lucrative Side Hustles*	206

CHAPTER 1

Time's Always Running Away

The 1964 cover version of the song *Time Is On My Side* by *The Rolling Stones* was memorable for its defiant rendition of the refrain *"yes, it is!"* Back then, who could have predicted that the band's frontmen, Mick Jagger and Keith Richards, will be alive today and still be performing, subject to a pacemaker or two? Ostensibly, it is unwise to judge a song - or singer - by its cover!

Is time an illusion? A youthful 20-year old Jagger might well have envisioned an endless stream of 20,000-plus hedonistic days ahead of him, whereas a crusty 75-year old Sir Mick, now counting down the years, must surely realise that time was no longer on his side. Whichever way you dice it, mortality is a brutal reality that limits the human life span to six score years or less.

Beyond our primordial perception of time, its measurement by instrumentation has evolved over several millennia. But since the *Age of*

Enlightenment, two near-immortal physicists - Isaac Newton and Albert Einstein - respectively, promoted a mathematical construction of time, and a more rigorous method of synchronising clocks relative to the speed of light. Because we are earthbound in a three-dimensional configuration, the scientific idea of space-time further illuminated the abstract concept of time, based on the spatial reference frame of the observer. Time's relentless little trick is to move us - in the blink of an eye - from a known space to an unknown territory. Try to navigate that!

However, to a layperson or gruff rocker, time is expressed more simply in the changing of the seasons, in the movement of the Sun and the Moon, but most visibly in the workings of a clock and a calendar.

So, what explains our obsession with time?

Simply put, all our thoughts and actions are delimited by time, which we can neither tame nor fully comprehend. Sometimes, the passage of time mimics a captive passenger on a high-speed train journeying to an unknown destination. But a more subdued objective reality correlates with our individual perception of the past, the present and the future.

The *past* embodies our achievements, failures, dashed dreams, and regrets. Also, we are a product of our antecedents, traditions and history, which represent a window into gaining an understanding of what worked in the past, and what to avoid going forward. Nevertheless, the past is not always a useful predictor since extrapolations into the future can result in statis or, worse, diminishing returns.

The *present* allows us to take stock of the past and to re-imagine the future. It provides an opportunity to take personal responsibility, to recalibrate and set audacious goals. Despite internal and external constraints, the present can inspire us to aim high, to make intelligent trade-offs and to seek the greatest value within our domain.

The *future* is full of potential and signifies an open book that is yet to be written. Having set goals, the effectiveness of our efforts or productivity prompts us to determine the efficiency of our portfolio of value-adding activities. Unlike machines, we have the uncanny ability to make micro-adjustments on the fly and to self-correct our actions in the pursuit of higher ideals.

Implicitly, the axiom *Time is Money* signals an economic motive, and also recognises the fact that time is a form of currency. This opens up the whole vista of effective time management and why we should not undervalue this precious resource. Put another way, we all need to explore how best to maximise the return on our time investment, in order to leave the world better than we met it.

Even as time shows us all a clean pair of heels, this blog will revisit and deconstruct a dogged and indispensable currency that never stops giving, from here to eternity.

CHAPTER 2

Hardly Simple

Simplicity

The word association between simple, simpleton and simplistic is psychologically indelible. It is, however, mystifying how a word that means easy is often conflated with being foolish and shallow, in that order. Sometimes, simple is also wilfully alternated with cheap and unsophisticated. Does this perhaps explain why technology companies, for instance, embraced the banal word *user-friendly* in the 1970s, rather than describe their products as easy to use?

To avoid getting lost in a semantics rabbit hole, I will adopt the utilitarian definition of simple as "*uncomplicated in form, nature or design.*" In contrast, the opposite word, complex, connotes "*difficult to analyse or understand.*"

On the surface, it would seem like an easy decision to favour simplicity over complexity, but that would disregard the true nature of the world. We live on a planet where people are constantly striving to create order out of chaos. Nonetheless, it is virtually impossible to remain at equilibrium because of life's tendency to tip us into chaos when we least expect it. In the same vein, the physical and metaphysical world that we inhabit is inherently complex, which leaves us with the abiding challenge of how to simplify our existence.

For now, instead of addressing existential questions, I will explore the correlation between simplicity, complexity and creativity, bearing in mind that human creativity and complexity are sometimes inseparable. To be sure, creativity is a very broad canvas that is associated with everything from an idea to a painting, musical score, conceptual design, scientific theory, and the list goes on. In practice, finding the sweet spot between complexity and simplicity is often difficult, and sometimes can prove elusive. But be that as it may, below are some non-dogmatic principles that you may find compelling in the pursuit of simplicity:

1. **Articulate** a vision and/or **Visualise** an outcome **Reduce** complexity by shrinking or hiding whatever is superfluous
2. **Subtract** the unnecessary and add discreetly
3. **Prioritise** and **Organise** with tact
4. **Embrace** openness and empty spaces
5. **Eliminate** waste and reap more from less
6. **Compress** time by removing non-value adding steps
7. **Concede** that complexity is sometimes unavoidable

On that last point, can you think of a situation when complexity might be inescapable? It may sound facetious, but who would want to travel in a spacecraft that couldn't lift off the launch pad?

For those who are decidedly earthbound, the stakes may not be as *high*, nevertheless logic suggests that a one-cap-fits-all design philosophy across the primary, secondary, service and knowledge sectors of the economy is hardly tenable. Therefore, when developing a product or service, it pays to keep the expectations of users or consumers

- delineated as expert, middlebrow and conventional - in firm focus.

Expert users are usually unfazed by complexity and viscerally demand new features, customisation, and a high degree of sophistication. *Middlebrows* will tolerate moderate changes from the norm, but within touching distance of their comfort zone. The majority of people, portrayed as being *conventional*, expect few frills and are motivated primarily by functionality, simplicity, and affordability.

Two iconic products - Ford Motor's *Model T* vehicle and Apple's *iPod* music player - demonstrated how to succeed by appealing to the mass market without compromising quality. Intriguingly, a counterintuitive finding over the years has shown that it is often more difficult to build a simple and robust product that works than to develop a complex alternative.

Simplicity may lack high salience but undervaluing it is usually a losing proposition.

CHAPTER 3

Energy Blues

Former US President Richard Nixon, a hard-boiled conservative, signed the landmark *Clean Air Act (1970 CAA)* into law nearly half a century ago. Today, his fellow Republicans are contemptuous of scientific evidence for human-induced climate change. And long before the party's 2008 vice-presidential candidate, Sarah Palin, threw red meat to her base by sneering *Drill, Baby, Drill,* a would-be American anarchist, Bill Epton, had coined the street-level battle cry *Burn, Baby, Burn*.

Even as the push for renewable energy intensifies, right-wing ideologues brandish their licence to drill and burn more coal, oil and natural gas. Capitalist boors notwithstanding, the gravest global challenge this century may well be how to manage the competing interests of the rich West and those that Harvard historian Niall Ferguson referred to as the *Rest*.

Two hundred and fifty years after the *Industrial Revolution* laid the foundation for the rise of the West's middle class, we are at the cusp of witnessing a much larger cohort. To power this expansion, the world's energy needs will most definitely rise by a prodigious order of magnitude.

First, dispelling a spellbinding age-old fantasy, the laws of thermodynamics have quashed the quest for a perpetual motion machine which, if it ever existed, would produce 'free' energy. In the real world, the sources of energy are, in fact, twofold - non-renewable and renewable.

Non-renewable energy refers to conventional fuels that drive the modern economy but have also been responsible for appalling environmental pollution. Fossil fuel reserves are finite in scope and will eventually run out at the current rates of exploration, but maybe not soon enough.

By contrast, renewable or alternative energy is much more sustainable because of its reliance on classical and natural processes. Broadly, alternative energy sources are classified as solar, wind, geothermal, tidal, hydrogen, biomass, wave and hydroelectric. Although nuclear power produces relatively clean energy, it is highly controversial due to extreme waste disposal and safety concerns.

By and large, I discern three distinct interest groups, namely energy cynics, energy romantics and energy pragmatists.

Energy cynics tend to live in the moment. Ignoring any potential moral hazard, they espouse the rationale that natural resources exist to facilitate economic growth. To them, marketplace success trumps ecological and moral considerations.

Energy romantics are sometimes dismissed as apocalyptic naysayers, who are predisposed to singing the blues. To their credit, they highlight the causality between greenhouse gas emissions and global warming, the risks from nuclear power, as well as the cumulative effects of environmental decay.

Energy pragmatists, on their part, contend that fossil fuels still constitute about 85% of net global energy production. They acknowledge the tremendous progress on the renewable energy front and the positive effect on the climate, but seem to hedge their bets about how quickly we should wean the world off carbon-based fuels.

According to a report by the *International Renewable Energy Agency (IRENA),* renewable energy will be consistently cheaper, as a source of electric power generation, than traditional fuels by 2020. That is the good news, unless you are an oil and gas producer. Unfortunately, alternative energy resources are not always available where and when they are needed, as typified by solar and wind power which are intermittent by nature.

Inevitably, this brings up the issue of energy storage. Storage batteries, because of their density and applicability, still account for the bulk of the market. Other solutions include compressed air, flywheel, and pumped hydro, but none of these comes close to matching the energy density of fossil fuels.

From the foregoing, it is clear that balancing the complexity of energy resourcing with economic realities and climate change imperatives is fiendishly difficult. Can we trust politicians to do right by us? And while we dither, would we know when the climate has reached a tipping point?

I invite all *energy realists* to contribute to the ongoing sustainability debate in ways large and small.

CHAPTER 4

Ma Lessons

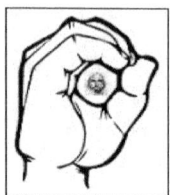

As a mental puzzle, I wonder how much time an average person spends each day thinking about nothing. For the next couple of minutes, I urge you not to switch off because I will, in fact, be writing about nothing.

Broadly, and depending on the context, nothing is analogous to zero, empty, void, or zilch. Of the lot, perhaps none has a more colourful history than zero which, paradoxically, was invented to fill a mathematical void.

Like most things that we take for granted, there was a world *before* and *after* the symbol zero replaced a generic placeholder adopted by early civilisations. Credit for the invention of numerical zero goes to ancient India, from where it travelled to China, and then to the Middle East, before reaching Europe via Spain in the 11th century. Initially frowned upon by church leaders, who considered zero to be preposterously "satanic" and disruptive, nevertheless it became a useful tool for doing arithmetic and later gained favour among medieval merchants. Without zero, it is conceivable that the world of negative numbers, calculus, physics, engineering, economics and computers might not exist, at least not as we know it.

Almost as bizarre as the idea of zero is the Japanese concept of *Ma*. Just as algebraically-challenged people struggle to comprehend negative numbers, *Ma* embodies the notion of negative space and feeds into the Japanese psychic reverence for empty space. By definition, negative space is the void that exists within, between and around objects. You will be forgiven if you thought that *Ma* sounds like a new age contrivance. In reality, it has deep-rooted resonance on a cramped island nation where physical space is at a premium.

In simple terms, *Ma* connotes "*not things, but the space between them.*" This embrace of emptiness or negative space naturally found its way into Japanese architecture, landscape design, art, poetry and music, and has gradually seeped into the Western brand of minimalism.

So, how much has *Ma* penetrated Western consciousness? It is hard to tell. However, I am very intrigued by the British movement known as *Meanwhile Space*. Its stated mission is to "*bring temporarily redundant space into productive use and to unlock underused space for enterprise and community cohesion.*" In recent years, the glacial displacement of hundreds of high street shops in the UK by online retailers has gained negative momentum. In the wake of this unsettling transformation, the founders of *Meanwhile Space* conceptualised the *ma*_rvellous idea of *ma*_ximising the value of vacant, negative spaces between storefronts.

Meanwhile Space provides a brilliant peekaboo illustration of how to interact with empty space. Creatively, value can indeed be extracted from a void without permanently impinging on a bias to leave it bare. We should also remember that the non-materiality of an empty space does not imply that it should be disturbed, if the imposed activity is non-value adding.

From a human perspective, a *Ma* mindset teaches us to avoid physical and psychological clutter in our everyday lives. But just as nature presumably abhors a vacuum, there are people who experience kenophobia, or the fear of empty spaces. Closely related to the fear of solitude, sufferers often resort to therapy or anti-anxiety medications. For the vast majority who are non-sufferers, *Ma* poses the enduring challenge of how to master space without being overly intrusive.

All in all, the power of nothing is incontrovertible and, if you'll pardon the syntax mishmash, never ever take nothing for granted. Surely, your dutiful Ma must have told you that.

CHAPTER 5

The Coming Revolution

Two of the world's most celebrated works of art, *David* and the *Pietà*, were sculpted at the turn of the 16th century by Michelangelo, the Florentine outlier. Michelangelo chipped away at massive blocks of Tuscany marble like an ordinary artisan wielding a hammer and chisel. However, only an extraordinarily gifted artist could have divined such masterpieces.

Fast-forward to the 19th century when the flowering of culture had given way to a more rational and technical era, typified by the invention of the milling machine. This trailblazing tool was used to shape solid objects by removing excess material to form an end product. Subsequently, the *Machine Age* ushered in machines that automated physical tasks for high-volume mass production. The

Digital Age, just decades old, introduced machines that automate mental tasks in the form of computer software.

Some have wondered where the Michelangelos and Leonardo da Vincis of our age are likely to be found. *Silicon Valley,* perhaps? If instantiated, that would represent quite a wild ride for two archetypal *Renaissance* men mutating into Californian software engineers! Generally acknowledged as history's most towering genius, the thought of Leonardo da Vinci interfacing with modern gadgets beggars the imagination.

These days, software innovation is gradually shifting focus away from subtractive to additive manufacturing. Traditional manufacturing techniques are based on mechanised labour subtracting material from a larger block to create a prototype, a moulding tool, or a finished product. Tellingly, a significant drawback in subtractive manufacturing is that as much as 90% of the base material is wasted, when not recyclable.

Starting in the 1980s, additive manufacturing or 3D Printing (3DP, three-dimensional printing) began its slow ascent to a potential tipping point in terms of adoption. To the uninitiated, 3DP encompasses the technologies and processes that enable production layer by layer - on a sub-micro scale - in an additive process. It starts with the design of a three-dimensional digital model of a product. Next, a generated 3D-readable file or blueprint is sent to a 3D printer which then translates base materials such as metals, plastics, food substrates, sand or ceramics into a prototype or a final product.

Early adopters included the medical and dental sector where personalisation of human parts such as hip implants, hearing aids and dental crowns was dominant. The architectural, space exploration, automotive, aerospace, fashion, and jewellery industries could also justify the high 3DP set-up costs in the pursuit of high-value bespoke customisation. Once a niche market, the exploitation of 3DP by smaller organisations and individuals began when the price point of an entry-level 3D printer dipped below US$1,000.

As additive manufacturing became more democratised, the new technology slowly migrated from the fringes to the mainstream. For conservationists who champion resource efficiency in manufacturing, 3DP guarantees negligible material and energy loss. Furthermore, industrial 3DP eliminates the need for dedicated tools and the associated factory expenditure. Therefore, as a contribution towards the long-term health of our planet, this is a big deal.

Aside from the manufacturing-on-demand efficacy of 3DP, other advantages include localisation, product personalisation, nimbleness, affordability, and faster prototyping. Since a product design file can be transmitted to a 3D printer anywhere in the world, supply chains will routinely be bypassed and disaggregated. In addition, reduction in product stockpiling will drastically lower storage and transportation costs.

On the downside, two headline threats to the growth of additive manufacturing must be addressed. First is the issue of counterfeiting and intellectual property infringement. Unless practitioners are able to protect their copyrights, this may curb innovation. Equally worrisome is the unintended latitude afforded private citizens to manufacture dangerous weapons like guns and knives. Already, regulators may well be behind the curve.

It's a safe bet that 3DP will not wholly supplant subtractive manufacturing, but rather complement it. As a budding proposition, additive manufacturing seems poised to revolutionise sustainable production, supply chains, the job market, and much more. Stay tuned.

CHAPTER 6

Parched Parched Parched

Can you tell the difference between *Wet, Wet, Wet* and *Wet Wet Wet*? I imagine that the former presupposes that by ducking and weaving, you could avoid the worst of an onrushing shower if you ran into the nearest shelter. On the other hand, *Wet Wet Wet* suggests that you are already soaked to the skin in a blinding rainstorm. As a graduate student, it was perhaps curious that my *Bob Dylan* initiation coincided with my first encounter *Wet Wet Wet*, a 1980s Scottish rock band. Their contrasting musical styles echoed the personalities of the dour Dylan and the latter's gregarious lead vocalist, Marti Pellow, who sported an improbably coiffed pompadour.

Discordantly, there is no discernible difference between *Parched, Parched, Parched* and *Parched Parched Parched*, since both convey unforgiving desolation, distress and barrenness. Parched means bone dry which, at myriad levels, paints a most terrifying picture of human deprivation.

The world has come a lot way since great rivers such as the Nile, Tigris, Euphrates, Tiber, Yangtze, and Indus catalysed agriculture and early human civilisations. In contrast, arid regions have struggled throughout history and many continue to be blighted by water shortages. Inarguably, the relative peace, prosperity and stability of many parts of the world have been shaped by water politics and internecine land disputes. The correlation between water and the ecology of life on Earth could hardly be overstated. By and large, we all live in unconscious awe of water, without which life as we know it could not exist. At the most basic level, access to clean water is supposed to be a universal human right, but is it?

With a bang, the 20th century witnessed a rapid increase in population growth, industrialisation and technological advances, as well as massive improvements in sanitation, healthcare, and access to safe drinking water. The emergence of a truly global middle class, now including hundreds of millions of Chinese, Indians, and large swathes of the southern hemisphere, ignited a new industrial revolution which, in turn, sparked an unprecedented scramble for strategic resources, including water. Given that no one could reasonably argue against human progress, the unintended consequences of rampant pollution, encroaching desertification, severe drought, and the damaging effects of climate change inevitably rose to the top of the global agenda.

Meanwhile, poor governance, mismanagement and corruption have hampered the availability and supply of healthy water to over one billion people worldwide, while global supply of fresh water is projected to decrease by as much as 30% in the coming decades.

So, as the world's population rises inexorably to 9-odd billion by mid-century, how worried should we be about water scarcity, as unrelenting demand pressure continues to mount on this most strategic natural resource? Can we moderate our water consumption by generating more from less through recycling, optimal pricing and water efficiency regulations? Furthermore, are there more focused strategies that can help protect the hydrosphere, in order to conserve our groundwater, lakes, streams, rivers and oceans?

To mitigate an impending crisis despite baffling scepticism in high places, practical interventions are available in the GlobeScan and SustainAbility Poll summary published by more than 1,200 leading international experts from 80 countries.

CHAPTER 7

Law and Other

As a 14-year old student, Newton's Third Law of Motion ***For every action, there is an equal and opposite reaction**/ represented a higher gear shift for an impressionable if fledgling scientist. Much later, I discovered that many non-scientists were vaguely familiar with this law, seemingly appropriated into general lexicon.

At university, I was awestruck by Heisenberg's Uncertainty Principle ***The more precisely the position of a quantum particle is determined, the less precisely its momentum can be known, and vice versa**/. But unlike Isaac Newton's deterministic world, the field of quantum mechanics is highly probabilistic, and so fuzzy as to preclude whimsical allusion.

As a third-tier staff analyst enthralled by owning a personal computer, I stumbled upon Moore's Law ***The processor speed, or the number of transistors in an integrated circuit, will double every two years**/. In those days, new computer models were launched in virtual lockstep with ever more powerful microprocessors, based on Gordon Moore's groundbreaking prediction. Though unrelated, I also recall the first time I encountered Pareto's Law ***For many events, roughly 80% of the effects come from 20% of the causes**/.

As an engineer turned management consultant, it struck me that the rigorous characterisation of a scientific law, requiring reproducible data or mathematical proof, was blithely being usurped by the business community. From the perspective of science purists, Moore's Law is highly contrived. A careful analysis of Werner Heisenberg's Principle perhaps confirms why more cautious professionals chose to express Pareto's Law as *Pareto Principle* or the *80/20 Rule*.

The *80/20 Rule (Pareto) is* attributed to the late 19th century Italian economist, Vilfredo Pareto, who unearthed the fact that 80% of his country's land was owned by 20% of its citizens. Since then, *Pareto* has been applied in a broad cross-section of human endeavours - from economics, engineering, computing, and healthcare to sports. In reality, the percentages can shapeshift, with the critical variables ranging from 10% to 30%; that is, 90/10 to 70/30.

Incidentally, the most quoted version of *Pareto* states that 80% of sales come from 20% of clients. Another ascribes 80% of a company's total production to 20% of its workforce. As a basic principle, *Pareto* advises managers to focus their time on 20% of what truly matters, and underscores why *Pareto* is sometimes called the principle of the *"vital few and trivial many."*

Within the derogatory *"trivial many"* phrase lies the challenge and anticipated pushback at what seems like a confirmation bias for hierarchical structures. There are those who would clamour for an equitable or balanced 50/50 outcome, in principle. The response to that ideology is simple. Societies where equality of outcome has been pursued by fiat have usually witnessed egregious tyranny. By contrast, a free but imperfect system strives to create a level-playing field and equal opportunity for all. However, with all the best intentions in the world, merit-based systems are just as susceptible to corruption and power play.

In essence, Pareto's prescient observation provided ample evidence that no society or human organisation is infallible, or remotely utopian. Notwithstanding, if a nation's goal is to achieve long-term prosperity, it is essential that the most competent people or the *"vital few"* are motivated to produce maximally, while the *"trivial many"* are unimpeded in realising their full potential. Unfortunately, the price for such pragmatism is an inevitable pyramid structure.

While a physical law imposes universal *order* on natural phenomena, Pareto's *80/20 Rule* falls short of that standard. Yet, the global impact of the *othèr,* lesser paradigm is just as consequential.

CHAPTER 8

Zero-Sum Delusion

Professor John Nash received the Nobel Prize in 1994 for his contribution to the field of game theory, the premise of the *zero-sum game*. A couple of years later, the movie *A Beautiful Mind* featured Russell Crowe as Nash spiralling into schizophrenia in an ironic twist to the film's title. Emotionally wrenching in parts, the dramatisation of John Nash's life may have led some viewers to infer that genius is not cost-free.

Equating stereotypical mathematical brilliance to eccentricity, or worse, is a hunch that is often off the mark. No less misleading is the analysis of the *zero-sum game* which, at its most cynical, asserts that for one faction to win, the opposing side must be crushed. Cue the mythical TV series *Game of Thrones* in which noble families vie to control the

Seven Kingdoms and the Iron Throne, such that you either win or die trying.

Another illustration of a *zero-sum game* is provided by the classic pastime *Monopoly* in which the amount of money, and associated properties, is constant. Since new assets are not created, one participant's loss or missed opportunity is another player's gain. Presumably, this represents an indulgent case where a resentful loser can contemplate, but just about refrain from, throttling the winner.

In real-life, liberal economics is more nuanced, by skewing towards a ***positive-sum game*** or a *win-win* outcome. By leveraging trade, novel ideas and technological innovation, economies can create *something from virtually nothing*, as new value generates additional wealth. In this scenario, it would be wrong to imply that individuals only get richer at the expense of others. In fact, an expanding economic pie ensures that the majority can come out ahead.

Geopolitics offers an unsettling instance of a ***negative-sum game***, whereby all participants end up on the losing side. Ever since the nuclear genie was let out of the bottle, the world has lived in the shadow of total annihilation. At the height of the *Cold War*, a nihilistic technocrat coined the term *mutually assured destruction*, a mad phrase that conveys the certainty of synchronised genocide in the event of a nuclear exchange between the US and the former Soviet Union (now Russia).

Less destructive than the *lose-lose* fallout of an inconceivable nuclear war, but equally insidious, is the manifestation of a ***zero-sum delusion*** typified by a "*we win-you lose*" environmental strategy often pursued in plain view. As the world has grown more prosperous, the disposal of unprecedented levels of waste has heightened the basest of human instincts through "*blight-thy-neighbour*" policies.

To be clear, waste materials are not created equal. Some are inert while others are degradable. Many are benign whereas some are extremely toxic. At one end are those that comply with the dictum *"dust to dust"* by decomposing and returning to nature. At the other extreme are nuclear wastes. Consider the startling fact that the half-life (*the time it takes for an isotope's radioactivity to decay to half its original value*) of Uranium-234 released from spent fuel rods is 245,000 years. Years not hours! As such, securing radioactive wastes from nuclear power plants presents a huge dilemma.

Though less alarming, electronic waste or e-waste from discarded digital appliances poses an increasing pollution challenge. While strands of e-waste are recyclable, harmful materials like lead and cadmium that usually end up in distant landfills remain hazardous. Nowadays, countries that send their trash to developing nations are being called out in the media; for instance, here and here. For decades, our oceans and marine life have been heaving and groaning under direct assault from plastics and other non-biodegradable products. While climate change has swamped the airwaves, the dominant attitude in waste management has devolved into a feckless howl of *"not in my backyard!"*

In the long run, all parochial attempts to deflect or fend off hydra-headed threats may prove futile since, by and large, every neighbourhood is a potential *Ground Zero*.

CHAPTER 9

Déjà Vu?

The generations born after World War II could be forgiven for believing that economic growth was their birthright. Nowadays, intrinsic metrics for human progress have come to include *faster*, *always on*, *more abundant*, *thinner*, *more liberal*, *cheaper* or, better still, *free*. As these and similar expectations ratchet up in a frenzied and hyper-connected world, perhaps a little perspective is in order.

Until about 200 years ago, agrarian societies relied on animate energy and power provided by water and wind. In a labour-intensive but low productivity era, the daily routine for most of humanity was to rise, work up a sweat, till the land, and anticipate a good harvest. Today, how many people are aware that 50 years after the United

States of America gained independence, China's GDP was about 18 times the size of the US economy and represented a third of global economic output? India's was about half China's size, but was equivalent to the combined GDP of Great Britain, France, Spain and Germany! At this point in history, the peak GDP per head was less than US$2.0 per day.

In the 18th century, the first textile mills in the UK increased productivity a hundredfold and massively destabilised British weavers and hosiers. Consequently, proprietors took advantage of mechanisation by reducing wages and employing unskilled machine operators, thus raising the tension between the owners of capital and workers. In the event, demands for higher pay, as well as for better working and living conditions, were ignored or repressed. In response, this led to arson, riots and, for posterity, great English poetry.

This phase of industrialisation turned out to be a mere prelude to what was to follow. The refinement of the steam engine in the 19th century improved the design and efficiency of pumping machines, waterwheels, windmills and rail transportation. But the epic game-changer was the internal combustion engine, which represented a remarkable *inflection point* in human history. This invention led to pistons generating motive force *on steroids*, thereby boosting productivity and turbocharging industrial growth throughout the 20th century. The car industry indirectly spawned the suburb, aviation blurred distances, telecommunications streamlined information flow, rocketry landed the first man on the Moon, and corporations transformed all facets of life.

With the advent of assembly lines and factory automation, predictions of mass unemployment became rife. However, the spread of secondary and university education, surprising innovations during gruesome wars, and economic development upended the most dire forecasts. In the process, capitalism may have become a victim of its own success, with opponents and critics quick to highlight its flaws.

In a shrunken world, poor and fleet-footed people everywhere want what others have, unlike in the past when just about everyone was poor and few knew what transpired beyond their immediate community. Furthermore, as income inequality has widened, the idea that people would readily accept stagnating living standards, like they did prior to the 18th century, seems quaint.

At the beginning of the 21st century, the post-industrial age is signalling the long-anticipated coming-of-age of Artificial Intelligence (AI) and genetic engineering. Under the searchlight of sophisticated algorithms, machine learning, additive manufacturing, gene-editing technology, and advanced robotics, unparalleled efficiency gains could emerge. While no one is certain what a new economic order will look like, the impact of data as a resource is expected to be as pervasive as the imprint of oil and the internal combustion engine over a century ago.

Meanwhile, the creative destruction of whole industries continues unabated. In the ensuing makeover, let us hope that the floundering hands and idle feet of the dispossessed do not steer them into the devil's workshop. Banish the thought, but could we finally be running out of road in creating high-quality middle-class jobs, with the rapid shift from an industrial to a knowledge-based economy? Yet, we could be witnessing another expectation-defying *paradigm shift* driven by digital propulsion.

Looking ahead as an adventurous species, it seems that we have the capacity to keep innovating until we encounter the limits of the laws of nature, we might even colonise Mars, but should we expect economic growth in perpetuity against all odds?

>>>>><<<<<

CHAPTER 10

Joe & Jo Pleb

Before the industrial age, the majority of human beings worked on the land. Without access to machines, labourers and farm animals alike were fed from harvested crops, thereby depleting outputs and reducing agriculture to a subsistence enterprise. At that time, the plebeian class also included craftsmen, miners, hunters, fishermen, and foot soldiers, who literally had to win the bread that kept their families alive. On their part, women's childcare and housekeeping chores were deemed as necessary, but insufficient, exertion that fell short of being acknowledged as bona fide work.

Before exploring the *future of work*, it may be useful to highlight the genesis of the unconscious bias between the respective roles of men *(archetype*

Joe) and women *(avatar Jo)*, based on the long association of work with strength. Since men are physically stronger than women (who, on average, possess about 40% less upper body strength), it was no surprise that men did much of the heavy lifting. And for those who believe that the concept of work is a patriarchal construct, remember that Newtonian physics defines work as the product of force and distance or the *"energy required to move an object through the action of a force."*

With that in mind, the vast majority of the industrial jobs created in exploration, manufacturing, construction, and other heavy industries were tailor-made for men. On the other hand, women were relegated to less muscular occupations such as healthcare, catering, secretarial and back-office administration. Therefore, in a world of work that rewarded physicality, men had a built-in and, most certainly, unfair advantage.

Effectively tethered to the homestead, women had limited career opportunities until they gained access to birth control methods in the 1960s, and started benefiting en masse from higher education. By then, the domain of science, technology, engineering and mathematics *(S.T.E.M.)* was already dominated by men. Arguably, even if your average

Joe had a natural preference for the *S.T.E.M.s*, there was no denying the fact that he had a commanding head-start that may have discouraged a not-so-average *Jo* from pursuing such disciplines. So, while swaggering *Joe* flaunted his physical prowess and intelligence quotient *(IQ)*, *Jo* seemed to exhibit better communication skills and higher emotional intelligence quotient *(EIQ)*.

Modern-day culture warriors might justifiably be aghast at the thought of perpetuating stereotypical differences between the sexes. No doubt, the last half century witnessed unprecedented assimilation of women into formerly male-dominated professions, including the military. Nonetheless, studies conducted in countries where the greatest advances have been made in terms of gender equality showed that women are, by choice, still disinclined to become bricklayers or engineers.

Self-evidently, the tides of history seem to be turning against men in the workplace, stemming from the digital revolution. Starting with the automation of routine jobs traditionally undertaken by blue-collar workers, algorithmic technology is now encroaching on cognitive tasks performed by white-collar professionals. Even the military, another male bastion, is not exempt, as drones and autonomous fighting machines gain traction.

With the rise of the so-called gig economy, an increasing number of jobs now tend to be short-term, no-guarantee contracts. In the US, for example, as many as 3.5 million men work in the road transportation sector, including truckers and *Uber* drivers. Here's a recurring question: what would happen to all these people when self-driving vehicles go mainstream, since not everyone is a potential software engineer or data scientist? As automation intensifies around the world and wages begin to equalise, the challenge of keeping millions, possibly hundreds of millions, of people gainfully employed and well-remunerated will not recede.

For now, it is predicted that vocations such as nursing, social care, teaching, and other so-called pink-collar jobs like counselling and event management, which women dominate, are precisely those that may be least susceptible to digitisation. So, with a nod to the post-millennial generation - *Joe Pleb* step aside for *Alex Blog*, and *Jo* say ciao to *Alexa*. Now, does anyone have a clue what the cool jobs of the future will look like?

>>>>><<<<<

CHAPTER 11

Jack Ma's Catch-22

An unconventional leader of the People's Republic of China, Deng Xiaoping, set in motion market-driven economic reforms in 1978 after almost thirty years of orthodox Communist rule. That same year, Jack Ma was a 14-year old self-taught English tour guide who bootstrapped his way to a college degree ten years later.

In 1988, China's GDP had doubled to $US312 billion and by 2018 had shot up to a dizzying US$13.6 trillion! Meanwhile, Ma went from being an English teacher to building websites for Chinese companies, before co-founding in 1999 a business-to-business portal named Alibaba. In 2018, when he announced that he would step down as the Executive Chairman of the Alibaba Group, Ma had become one of the wealthiest entrepreneurs in China, worth over US$35 billion. In essence, Ma's remarkable success mirrored China's extraordinary rise as the world's second largest economy.

In April 2019, Jack Ma stirred up a hornet's nest when he publicly endorsed the so-called *996* work schedule. This proposes that workers should work from 9:00 a.m. to 9:00 p.m., six days a week. As one of the world's most influential business leaders, Ma's views were internationally parsed and debated, with many criticising him for claiming that "*employees who worked longer hours will get the rewards of hard work*." Even within China, where the labour law stipulates a 5-day schedule and no longer than 44 hours, many pushed back. Mostly post-millennials *(PMs)*, this is a generation drawn from China's one-child policy, which is perceived to be relatively coddled and opinionated.

Comparatively, *PMs'* grandparents, who lived through the social, economic and political upheaval fomented by the *Great Leap Forward (1958-61)* and the *Cultural Revolution (1966-76),* had indelible memories of extreme deprivations. During a period characterised by central planning and collectivisation, even Confucian values - which had steered China for over 2,000 years - were jettisoned.

However, by the late 20th century, *Confucian work ethic* had made a comeback when *PMs'* parents propelled China's rapid economic growth. Predicated on the principles of hard work, loyalty, frugality, skills acquisition and education, and submission of individuality to social harmony, it was argued by some Western *Protestant work ethic* advocates that the Confucian emphasis on collective achievement, rather than individual initiative, might hinder China's economic development.

In reality, blessed with an educated and diligent workforce, China became an economic powerhouse through structural reforms, infusion of foreign direct investment, and the replacement of Marxist-Leninist economic dogma with market tenets.

Now needing to reduce rural-urban inequality and to keep growing the ranks of the middle class, China faces the challenge of shifting to consumption-led growth and migration to high value-added industries. That being the case, should China be seeking to work longer and harder, or smarter?

To my mind, Jack Ma's *996* rallying cry portends the steamrollering of China into a *Catch*-22 cul-de-sac, as though this dynamic nation would forever remain the world's workshop. In any case, most

Chinese workers already work harder than their counterparts elsewhere and, inevitably, low-end production will relocate to developing nations that offer cheaper labour. And, according to John Pencavel of Stanford University, "*the relationship between hours worked and productivity found that employee output falls sharply after a 50-hour work-week, and falls off a cliff after 55 hours.*"

Incidentally, discussions about China's work culture has coincided with brewing trade tensions with the US, exemplified by the furore involving Huawei, a flagship Chinese company. Significantly, some analysts have described the attempt by US trade hawks to decouple the supply networks binding the world's two largest economies as China's *Sputnik moment* (analogous to when the US doubled down after the Soviet Union launched the first space satellite, *Sputnik 1*). Faced with this watershed moment, what should China do?

While acknowledging that access to natural resources will remain a strategic preoccupation, the *war for human talent* may be of greater significance. With 1.4 billion people, China produces the largest pool of engineers per annum by a mile, but simultaneously the *Middle Kingdom* is contending with an ageing population. Consequently, China's focus should be on building world-class academic and research institutions to attract Nobel-class scholars, while also diversifying its talent pool.

Therefore, to achieve *more from less* writ large, China's *Catch*-phrases ought to be *superior creative talent, higher productivity,* and *cutting-edge innovation,* rather than pander to numeral *996* or *9-to-whatever.*

CHAPTER 12

Building Blocks

Driven by rational self-interest, human beings have always been drawn towards activities that create economic value. And over the last century, pioneers in scientific management techniques, such as time-motion studies, laid the groundwork for improving work methods in a manual, mechanised, and progressively digital world.

Technically, a series of work methods, or *process*, is defined as *"a sequence of actions undertaken to achieve a particular end."* Furthermore, a process comprises discrete *tasks* that generate a rate of output per unit of input, and understanding how work activities produce an outcome is fundamental to how businesses gain competitive advantage. Essentially, these building blocks of productivity growth depend on tasks being undertaken faster, error-free, and cheaper without sacrificing quality.

With this backdrop, the foundation for process innovation rests squarely on the quote attributed to the late management visionary, Peter Drucker, who stated that *"what gets measured, gets managed"* or *"if you can't measure it, you can't improve it."* Now almost a cliché, when Drucker published this insight in 1954, the mechanical tools that would undergird performance measurements were very rudimentary. Still, many companies adopted a continuous improvement mindset and sought opportunities to establish baseline data, against which they could then track progress.

As automation capabilities expanded, sensors and productivity tools became more miniaturised and smarter, as did the ability of businesses to measure and improve efficiency. During this initial phase - *Process Innovation 1.0*, increasingly sophisticated computer technology boosted productivity, and induced the streamlining and periodic realignment of companies' organisational structures. Essentially, businesses hunkered down to compete for market share by leveraging key performance indicators and metrics such as speed of processing, cost efficiency, quality consistency, and customer satisfaction.

Expectedly, there are always exceptions to the rule. Luxury brands, for example, do not necessarily compete based on speed or price; rather, high marketing costs are expended for brand-building. By contrast, for the majority of large and small businesses, most of their products and services are commodities that attract low to modest margins. Under such circumstances, whether operating online or offline, process differentiation can be a winning strategy.

Unsurprisingly, hordes of management thinkers jumped on the process improvement and quality management bandwagon. Concepts such as *Business Process Reengineering (BPR)*, and *Six Sigma* infiltrated the business ranks and instigated an explosion of *How-To* books. On the shop floor, the sales department, the back office, and within core business functions, management consulting firms introduced performance metrics to assess how well companies were meeting their set targets. Before long, cross-industry best practices became widely available, and enabled businesses to benchmark their internal processes against global standards for improved performance. As an illustration, *BPR* entails the radical overhaul of value chains, the elimination of non-value-adding activities, and bold implementation of information technology solutions.

Shadowing the decades-long productivity push was the migration from mainframe to mini to personal computers, local to wide area networks and, ultimately, the invention and growth of the Internet. Advances in enterprise collaboration software also created a platform for better in-house communication and data-sharing. Externally, peak globalisation occurred as supply chain management, demand forecasting, contract management, and risk mitigation became ever more complex.

During this period, the volume of data generated grew exponentially, and data sets became more intractable. Process innovation, like many other spheres of business, is being re-imagined in the wake of new analytical tools, and emerging technologies such as 5G telecommunications networks, Internet of Things, and autonomous systems. As usual, the way forward would require thought leadership and creative disruption. It is still all to play for.

Ironically, a fly in the ointment has emerged just as multinational companies were gearing up for closer integration. The widening trade friction between major economic powers may be contained in the near term but, then again, it could trigger a de-coupling of supply networks, and a retreat into regional trade blocs. Not only will this not augur well for the global economy, it could cause a temporary slowdown in the evolution of *Process Innovation 2.0.*

CHAPTER 13

Visually Speaking

Crisp. Compact. Chic. Composed.

Silken. Spartan. Taut. Trim. Try *4C.2S.2T.*

But to what do these adjectives refer?

Before answering the question, first let me admit my ignorance but abiding fascination with an East Asian puzzle. To an untrained ear, hearing Mandarin or Cantonese spoken, say on TV, is always riveting. In print, the script is even more impenetrable.

Yet, on the few occasions when I have peered closely at the Chinese language script, instinctively I had a sense of *4C.2S.2T.* Really?? Honestly, I have never failed to admire its artistic flair, sphinx-like starkness, and beautiful brush strokes. Baldly stated, the ancient art of calligraphy largely credited to the Chinese has never lost its lustre. Aesthetically, I could not help but marvel at the luminous spacing, high density, and harmonious rendition of the characters, written from top to bottom, right to left, as if deliberately conceived to leave a Western-schooled mind permanently befuddled.

Representative of an ancient civilisation with a strong gravitational pull around the Pacific Rim, classical Chinese calligraphy was both a communication medium and an art form, which would later spread and influence Japanese, Korean and Vietnamese cultures. Written Chinese is made up of thousands of logographic characters (logograms) composed of parts that represent physical objects, abstractions, and syllables of spoken Chinese. Before the invention of paper, these symbols were engraved onto bone, shells and wood, and subsequently on silk, thus giving the medium very limited coverage.

To people unfamiliar with Far Eastern culture, thousands of years have barely diminished the scope of the *Chart of Common Characters of Modern Chinese*, which features about 3,500 logograms. Even today, Chinese students have to study and memorise as many as 2,500 characters to achieve basic literacy. In comparison, the Greek language has 24 alphabets, classical Latin 23, Arabic 28, Hebrew 22, modern English 26, and the Eurasian Cyrillic script 33. To be sure, although an English writer, for instance, has to learn only 26 letters, there are thousands of words that must be mastered to become truly proficient.

The degree to which classical Chinese calligraphy has influenced its Western sub-genre is open to conjecture. And while Chinese and Western languages are literally worlds apart syntactically and structurally, calligraphy as an artistic expression became a global phenomenon. As writing substrates evolved from tablets, scrolls, papyrus, and parchment to paper, Western calligraphers morphed into creative illustrators. Back then, only the powerful and wealthy could commission hand-bound illuminated manuscripts which, on average, took years to produce, and not least because of the cost and effort required to acquire the ink and writing materials.

In medieval times, the Roman Catholic Church exercised enormous political power and controlled the production and dissemination of religious codices in a highly hierarchical manner.

Subsequently, the invention of the printing press facilitated a network of book publishers which led to the democratisation of the printed word. Not all calligraphers were replaced by professional typesetters because a related craft emerged, which required the skill sets of typeface designers.

As printed books fostered the spread of formal education, typography became a specialised occupation within the publishing industry. In time, calligraphy was mainly associated with the creation of expressive inscriptions and ornate hand-lettering, and found application in the design of testimonials, event invitations, certificates, religious art, logos, and maps.

Calligraphy would continue to resonate in the fields of font design and graphic arts due to the outsized influence of the late co-founder of Apple, Steve Jobs. Somewhat fortuitously, legend has it that Jobs attended a calligraphy course offered by a former Catholic monk and academic, Robert Palladino, at Reed College. Jobs later said that, *"It was the first computer with beautiful typography. If I had never dropped in on that single course in college, the Mac would have never had multiple typefaces or proportionally spaced fonts."* Had Jobs not been an inveterate perfectionist and visionary,

Microsoft might well have foisted *Times New Roman*, *Sans Serif,* and a couple of generic fonts on us all.

Coming full circle from antiquity to now, calligraphy has provided the artistic inspiration for a lattice of beguiling typefaces in the digital age. To soothe today's harried souls, old-fashioned calligraphy perhaps offers a mode of *4C.2S.2T-*induced therapy for anyone willing to practise a timeless craft, requiring nothing more than a dip pen, writing ink, paper, and stillness in the limbs.

>>>>><<<<<

CHAPTER 14

Poor Earth

When Chinese President Xi Jinping toured a provincial rare-earth processing plant in May 2019, analysts speculated that his visit signalled overt messaging by China in the middle of tortuous trade negotiations with the US. Suspicions have long trailed China's near-monopoly over rare-earth supplies, not unlike the past scenario in the petroleum industry.

For decades, the Organisation of Petroleum Exporting Countries (OPEC) was viewed as a global arch-villain due to its cartel-like stranglehold on crude oil pricing. Ostensibly, if oil market shenanigans are embedded in consumers' psyche, the same could not be said about rare-earth metals (REMs). So, exactly what are they?

Rare-earth elements (REEs) refer to a group of 17 elements on the *Periodic Table* of similar chemical and physical properties. They are further subdivided into light (*e.g., Lanthanum*) and heavy (*e.g., Lutetium*) elements. Although there is a subliminal supposition that these raw materials are rare, in fact some are relatively abundant in nature but often in such low concentrations as to make mining them economically risky.

Primarily, rare-earth metals (or processed REEs) have applications in the high-technology sector. They are used sparingly as industrial catalysts, and in products such as mobile phones, flat-screen display panels, electric vehicle batteries, wind turbines, military weapons systems, and in low-carbon green technologies. Specifically, REMs are valued for their unique chemical, catalytic, magnetic, electrical and optical properties, thus designating them as strategic minerals.

The mining cycle of REEs is typically long, costly and environmentally perilous because ore deposits often contain radioactive isotopes, and less than 5% of ventures yield a producing mine. Total global production of REEs in 2018 was about 170,000 tonnes, with *China accounting for 70%,*

Australia 12%, the US 9%, Myanmar 3%, and Russia 1.5%.

If you've read this far, perhaps the narrative may seem as interesting as watching paint dry. Not only might REMs evoke repressed memories of high school chemistry, conceivably also of a 1980s alternative rock band. But try to hang on. Learning how the world's three largest economies - the US, China and Japan - are adjusting to the supply and demand of REMs might render invaluable geopolitical insights.

US: From a national security perspective, the US recognises how strategic REMs are to the de-carbonised technologies of the future. However, US investors and producers have to contend with market forces, as well as mining permits which can take upwards of 10 years to process. Given these disadvantages, the characteristic boom-and-bust nature of the global market for REMs favours Chinese producers and partly explains their dominance.

China: To quote China's former leader, Deng Xiaoping, *"The Middle East has oil. China has rare earths."* In 1992, Deng was alluding to the fact that China's 35% share of global reserves of rare earths was on a par with the Persian Gulf States' 36% control of proven oil reserves. Unlike their Western competitors who face onerous regulations, Chinese producers operate under fewer restrictions. Also, state-controlled mines benefit from Chinese government subsidies thus skewing world markets. As global demand grew, China tightened its control by introducing export quotas.

Japan: To a greater extent than the US, Japan is heavily import-dependent and has had to stockpile REMs over the years to meet domestic demand. Following a diplomatic dispute in 2010, China temporarily constrained the export of REEs to Japan. In the aftermath, natural resource-poor Japan has sought to reduce its vulnerability. Recently, Japanese scientists discovered seams of REEs within its territorial seabed in the Pacific Ocean, which would require innovative deep-sea mining techniques to extract.

As tit-for-tat protectionism and trade tensions mount, the US and its allies anticipate that China might leverage REEs as a bargaining chip. And although China's market share has dropped below a noose-tightening 95%, the barriers to replacing China as a supplier are very steep. To be clear, recycling REMs is not a serious option because they exist in manufactured products in such minute quantities; also, there are no obvious substitutes.

For all those who view the politics and economics of REMs through a low-resolution lens, they ought to pay particular attention to how the proposed ocean exploration of REEs will impact marine life and environmental standards. Recently, the *United Nations' International Seabed Authority* has begun to issue deep-sea mining licences to private companies, in the slipstream of the huge destruction caused by large mining corporations on land.

Regretfully, mineral exploration is intensifying in places that should remain pristine. On the 50th anniversary of man's first walk on the Moon, are we determined to turn our blue planet into another lifeless ball of goo?

CHAPTER 15

Alternative Intelligence

Standing in a queue at the *Louvre* museum in Paris, as it snaked towards arguably the most famous painting in the world, I was startled when an irreverent tourist out of my line of sight muttered, *"It is rather small, isn't it?"* Granted that the *Mona Lisa,* measuring *30in by 21in* seemed unimposing, nevertheless a 500-year degree of separation could not mask the lady's elegance and magnetic sheen. When in early 2019, I saw the ubiquitous image of *Mona Lisa* babbling animatedly in a *WhatsApp* clip, the surreal head and facial movements appeared clever but harmless.

Months later, another lady of Italian lineage, and the first female Speaker of the US House of Representatives, Nancy Pelosi, featured in an online video that portrayed her in a drunken state. Apparently, the image had been digitally doctored to show Pelosi stammering, and slurring her words. This occurred about two years after an aide to the incumbent US President deadpanned the insidious phrase *"alternative facts"* in a clumsy attempt to deflect the truth.

Welcome to the age of *deepfake* technology in the so-called post-truth world. Coming in the wake of the contentious 2016 US presidential elections when pernicious *fake news* infected social media, it has become increasingly difficult to separate accurate or factual information from the chaff of falsehood. For your information, *deepfake* derives from an image synthesis process, driven by artificial intelligence (AI), that many fear could become weaponised in the near future to undermine global institutions. Given today's toxic environment, the word "artificial" in AI is rather unfortunate and could be presumed to mean contrived, exaggerated or phony, which to an uncritical mind further erodes the legitimacy of digital platforms.

How did we stumble into *fake media*, and where could we possibly be heading? As a premise, there were about 26 million software engineers worldwide in 2019, representing about 0.34% of the global population. Therefore, on the subject of AI, the depth of technical knowledge accessible to over 99% of us is superficial at best. That said, consider the incredible fact that a smartphone, essentially a hand-held computer, is unimaginably more powerful than the system on board the Apollo 11 spacecraft! Fifty years after that historic launch, and after innumerable stops and starts, AI technology has finally begun late-stage testing of natural language processing, facial recognition, and self-driving cars. For better or worse, ready or not, and in the absence of common ethical and regulatory guidelines, AI is poised to reshape our future.

In retrospect, "artificial intelligence" was coined in 1955 not by a committee of experts but by John McCarthy, an inquisitive computer scientist. Although AI is sometimes referred to as machine intelligence, the term AI has stuck and seems embedded in our vocabulary. If McCarthy envisioned a machine that would mimic the brain's neural processes, in reality AI has progressed sufficiently to supplant the world champions of two strategic games, chess and Go - remarkable feats by any measure. However, AI faces huge challenges in replicating cognitive perception and dexterity reflective of human consciousness, which neuroscience still cannot explain. For instance, AI struggles to differentiate between high and low resolution objects, in order to infer meaning and derive understanding.

Coincidentally, the UK government this month honoured a former British computer pioneer, Alan Turing, by featuring his image on a currency note. He was famous for devising the *Turing Test* back in 1950, which is *"a test of a machine's ability to exhibit intelligent behaviour equivalent to, or indistinguishable from, that of a human."* Without delving too deeply into Turing's landmark challenge, AI capabilities have definitely grown in leaps and bounds, based on ground-breaking algorithms that facilitate self-learning by autonomous systems tapping into massive datasets.

So, should we be worried? Yes and No.

Yes, because I believe that AI technology has already developed to the extent of being able to fool human beings, examples of which include *fake news* and *deepfake* images. Furthermore, authoritarian governments and malevolent non-state actors are deploying AI-driven bots designed to confound and cause havoc in cyberspace. Whether liberal democracies will be able to repel this assault is an open question. Beyond that, who can predict what uninhibited, pimpled 17-year old programmers around the world might forge next?

No, because it is doubtful whether the agency exhibited by AI will ever match human cognition, that could enable a machine to, for example, tell a *"true"* lie. Irony aside, I believe that there is a gulf between a successful bluff and a whopping lie. Bluffing suggests a sleight-of-hand craft, practised most deftly by spies and poker players, in order to deceive and conquer. On the other hand, lying connotes a deep-seated and visceral human trait that implies that the perpetrator has something at stake worth protecting or hiding. Well, if machines ever develop contextual faculty to a degree that they routinely and convincingly lie to humans and other machines, then it could be curtains for the human species.

CHAPTER 16

Squeezed

The middle class is an ambiguous social construct inhabited by people best described as possessing *"significant human capital."* Their accrued potential places them a cut above the rank-and-file, but not in the same league as the privileged class. Typically, the middle class encompasses managers, salaried bureaucrats, small business-owners, and professionals who occupy the engine room of a modern economy. Decades-long access to skills training and knowledge resources led to unprecedented value-addition, wealth-creation, and improvements in living standards. Essentially, knowledge workers represent an indispensable backbone of civilised societies, with the tacit promise of upward mobility and a much-prized social status.

Although a thriving middle class is not an absolute precondition for a stable polity, it can serve as a bulwark against chaos. Also, it is undeniable that the health of a society can often be estimated by gauging the barometer of middle-class contentment or dissatisfaction. By that logic, it could be inferred that the middle class in many parts of the world is being buffeted from all sides by technological change, demographic flux, wage stagnation tied to globalisation, the effects of offshoring, and the capricious nature of international financial markets.

Consequently, the employment market is slowly shape-shifting into an hourglass configuration of a squeezed middle. Over time, this plasticity portends grave danger, with individual, national and global repercussions. Strong evidence of the structural transformation of labour markets means that a slew of skill sets that were perfectly relevant in the 20th century are becoming redundant in a post-industrial world.

With specific focus on the impact of technology on employment opportunities, the historical trend swung from agriculture and artisan labour, to manufacturing and management, and then service and virtuality. The automation of routine manual tasks in manufacturing, sales, marketing, and administrative support functions started the displacement of relatively low-paid, low-skilled workers through the substitution of human labour with machines and robots. Even the construction industry, which has sustained generations of workers, is moving towards prefabrication under controlled factory conditions. Increasingly, work-from-anywhere (or virtualisation), contract employment and *uberisation* are changing the work environment. The rare exceptions are the services provided by repairmen such as plumbers, carpenters and electricians, who perform irregular, non-routine tasks.

Recently, the computerisation of basic cognitive tasks like bookkeeping, data-processing, paralegal research, and several rules-based processes, using computer algorithms, has led to the gradual erosion of previously safe mid-range, white-collar job domains. As such, many middle-class employees are being pushed down to the lower rungs where they are now competing with low-paid workers in the service industry, often caricatured as generating retail and burger-flipping jobs.

Due to the current limitations of artificial intelligence, data analytics and robotics technology to replicate high-cognitive perception and manipulation tasks, certain mid-level jobs are largely exempt from automation. Such jobs comprise *creative intelligence tasks* like generating ideas, formulating scientific theories, writing poetry, and telling jokes. In this same category are *social intelligence tasks* that require persuasion, negotiation and human care skills.

Studies estimate that over 40% of mainstream employment is classified in the high-risk category, hence susceptible to automation over the next two decades. And as long as multinational companies continue to benefit from globalisation, capital will inevitably seek cheaper labour and more automation, thereby piling more pressure on middle-class wages.

With a hint of a smirk, at the top of the hourglass are jobs that demand sophisticated analytical, communication and problem-solving skills. As the hollowing-out of the middle class unfolds, only a fraction of well-educated but threatened workers will successfully move up the ladder. In addition, not everyone has the aptitude to slip into jobs that demand creative and social intelligence. Still, no one can predict the opportunities that a technology like additive manufacturing or 3D printing might engender, or the types of jobs that the build-out and maintenance of autonomous systems infrastructure would entail. While this technological makeover intensifies, are there any obvious solutions to the continuing polarisation of the labour market?

Progressively, workers should expect to work on multi-skilled, cross-disciplinary hybrid projects in interconnected and network-oriented mode. Furthermore, a seemingly implausible response may lie in the provision of often-overlooked vocational and technical training, championed by Germany, Austria, and a handful of other countries. Though much of what lies ahead is indecipherable, the apprenticeship model, with its emphasis on the acquisition of practical skills, may offer the flexibility to adapt and reposition for the future world of work.

To mitigate social pressure and fend off the rising tide of national populism, politicians need to pay urgent attention to the plight of the middle class. Inaction could precipitate disorder.

CHAPTER 17

Trust Me

Have you ever interacted with people who would feel embarrassed to admit that they watch television? I wonder what they would make of my unabashed disclosure of having binge-watched the critically-acclaimed television series *Breaking Bad* thrice! Chemistry was my favourite subject in school, which might partly explain my admiration for Bryan Cranston in the role of a cancer-stricken Chemistry teacher turned drug mastermind, nicknamed *Heisenberg*. Supported by his sidekick, former student Jesse Pinkman, and a superb cast of actors, *Walter White* discovered that he had the cold-eyed deftness for "cooking" methamphetamine *(crystal meth)*, an illegal recreational drug.

With a handful of murders under his belt and, after outwitting more seasoned criminal minds, *Walter White-Heisenberg* convinced himself that he *broke bad* for the sake of his young family. In the penultimate series episode, he ended up in an icy log cabin as a fugitive, with the assistance of Ed, an extractor-disappearer, who had provided him with a new identity and the safe house. In one of the most poignant exchanges of the series, a despondent and ailing *Walter White-Heisenberg* asked if Ed would ensure that his family received the balance of his fortune, north of $9 million, in the event of his death. Replied Ed, *"If I said yes, would you believe me?"* Needless to say, he did not, and plotted an alternative arrangement centred on two of his past tormentors.

A close study of *Walter White-Heisenberg's* preposterous and desperate request to Ed, an underworld character, illustrates the natural human inclination to trust others, often against our best judgment. Let us remember that, in a best-case scenario, trust is a very nebulous primordial instinct held in awe by psychologists, anthropologists, and others who study human nature.

Without mutual trust and cooperation, it is difficult to imagine how early human communities could have evolved into well-functioning and civilised societies. Since no one is an island, trust between two parties invites either party temporarily to give up control and rely on the competence and actions of the other party for a desired outcome. Statistically, the odds of both parties being satisfied or disappointed may vary anywhere from zero to one hundred per cent. As economic agents, in particular, trust is our most conspicuous calling card.

A good case study is the example of eBay, an online auction and shopping website. When the marketplace was launched in the mid-1990s, sceptics were quick to point out why it would fail. The general feeling was that *"if one party attempts to sell a defective item, the buyer would simply send a cheque primed to bounce."* Even with eBay's money-back guarantee backed by law-enforcement regulations, the risk that the platform would collapse under the weight of counterfeits and distrust remained high. As it turned out, eBay was one of the few start-ups that survived the carnage of the dot-com bubble. Would it be naive to ascribe eBay's surprising success to subscribers' altruism or innate trustworthiness? On the other hand, could it be due to individuals' desire to protect their reputation, or did eBay benefit from an environment that was predicated on the rule of law?

More broadly, a case could be made that a country with a relatively honest or ethical civil service and judiciary is infinitely more likely to prosper. By contrast, nations with corrupt institutions, weak law enforcement, low social trust, and uneven governance structures tend to stay poor and anarchic. Rampant skulduggery and lack of accountability are other hallmarks of venal and dysfunctional states. Clearly, there is no gainsaying the fact that economies thrive better in a transparent environment where reliability, predictability and security exist, and business confidence is high.

So, to these questions. *First,* are human beings inherently trustworthy or dishonest, and are we more likely to trust those with whom we share the same culture and values? *Second,* is there a correlation between poverty, scarcity, and untrustworthiness? *Third,* how much do peer reviews and legal agreements moderate business behaviour? *Fourth,* how effectively do spiritual and secular norms promote ethical practices? *Lastly,* what can be done to spread and entrench the benefits of a universal framework of good governance? Almost certainly, these and similar questions will continue to attract the attention of social scientists, game theorists and policymakers.

Plainly, the world of business could do with more trust-building measures, not less, since the future will always be uncertain. Though an intangible quality, trust represents an essential social capital and secret sauce of business success, by helping opposing parties manage expectations, transaction costs, and myriad contingencies.

All told, trust could be extremely fragile because, once lost, it can prove difficult to regain. And as a rule, if you encounter someone who plays fast and loose with the prefix *"Trust me,"* don't recoil. Such a glib red flag could be harmless but, then again, would you have any reason to question the integrity of a bespectacled high school science teacher?

CHAPTER 18

Cat On A Hot Tin Roof

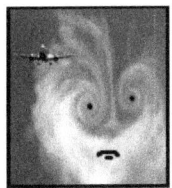

Aviation and turbulence are inextricably linked, and it is the rare traveller who has not experienced at least once that distinct stomach-churning sensation and overpowering jolt at 35,000 feet. Usually, the bumpiest ride is experienced by economy-class passengers at the rear of an aircraft, clearly the least desirable seat assignment for anyone susceptible to flight sickness.

Even for hardy types who are immune to motion sickness, or passengers fortunate to travel in the first-class cabin, being suspended in mid-air constitutes an uncomfortable, self-conscious if temporary, loss of control. The good news is that air transportation is as safe as it gets. However, flight turbulence can be both random and very scary.

Despite tremendous improvements in weather forecasting and predictive modelling, the arbitrariness of air turbulence is rooted in storms and rough jet streams at high altitude. Also, waves and wind currents propagated near high mountains can generate destabilising oscillations in the proximity of an airborne plane. Beyond aviation, fluid dynamics depicts turbulence as the rupture of laminar or streamlined flow of gases (or liquids) following a change in velocity, pressure and sundry factors.

To the highly inquisitive, turbulence generated near rough surfaces at the molecular or sub-atomic level can, in fact, enhance mass or heat transfer, whereby interface eddies aid material absorption or heat dissipation. I should know since that was my research topic. *To the mildly curious*, the transition from a simple steady state to the onset of turbulence can be transfixing - cue a rising plume of smoke gently turning into a tempestuous vortex when the intrinsic kinetic energy reaches a tipping point. *To the incurious*, turbulence is analogous to a *cat on a hot tin roof* - the antithesis of a calm, stable or restrained situation, and it is doubtful that anyone would welcome the presence of such a manic feline on their home turf. Try to picture an unhinged partner in a stormy marriage.

In truth, apart from scientists who probe subjects like turbulence, designated by the late Physics Nobel Laureate Richard Feynman as *"the most important unsolved problem in classical physics,"* very few people pay much heed to this natural phenomenon.

Subconsciously, we tend to associate turbulence with disorder and negativity. Consequently, at a personal level, it is intuitive to seek order in the midst of life's chaotic proclivities. At the macro level, perhaps nothing encapsulates turbulence more gravely than the tendency of nations to turn against each other. Generations who have lived through the nuclear age could be forgiven for assuming that relative global peace is the norm. In fact, decades of a cold, rather than hot, war between the world's great powers has been an historical aberration. In the past, Europe particularly witnessed intermittent conflicts that pitched nation-states against their neighbours, culminating in two tragic world wars. Today, regions like the Middle East or Central Africa remain hotbeds of turmoil and internecine warfare that, mercifully, have not ignited a wider conflagration.

Outside the realm of international politics, the business world also experiences periodic turbulence that features substantial risks as well as unforeseen opportunities. Economic turmoil comes in various guises, most commonly in the form of a recession, during which dominant players could be caught napping thereby giving smaller, more nimble rivals the opportunity to gain ground. If business cycles are a fact of life, an unusually **cat**aclysmic episode occurred during the *Great Depression* of the 1930s, when everything that could go awry went wrong. Protectionist policies, high unemployment, economic devastation, combined with toxic politics laid the groundwork for the horrors of World War II.

In 2008, the financial markets experienced a **cat**atonic meltdown triggered by the implosion of the US housing market. Many have described the ensuing *Great Recession* as a *black swan* event. Aside from such an unanticipated, bolt-out-of-the-blue crisis that blindsided just about everyone, economic turbulence can result from deliberate policy miscalculations. Presently, the ongoing trade friction between the US and China is straining and rocking the foundations of multilateral institutions built over several decades. Unless reason prevails, rhetorical brinkmanship may well induce trade ripples and overarching entropy, especially if China concludes that the US is attempting to suppress its rise as a global power.

Rather incongruously, a state of turbulence can sometimes dissipate as quickly as it appears, if *"the kinetic energy is converted into internal energy by viscous shear stress."* In other words, just as light follows darkness, eventually order tends to impose itself on mayhem. This suggests that human adversaries can lower tensions by pulling back and decelerating, as though walking through treacle, and wisely turn away from **cat**astrophic headwinds.

Meow!

CHAPTER 19

Social Division

Aired a couple of thousand years ago, these words may well be jarring to modern ears unaccustomed to old aphorisms: *"What has been will be again, what has been done will be done again; there is nothing new under the Sun."*

Today, digital social networks have taken centre stage and, like or loathe them, their in-your-face impact is inescapable; and whether they represent a force for good or ill remains an open question. To assess their value and what lies ahead, consider the following refracted view of the past.

From historical lore, the earliest recorded social network had precisely two members - Adam and Eve. To their eternal regret, they seemed oblivious to a reptilian eavesdropper lurking in the shadows, who must have overheard them mulling over the *"forbidden fruit."* As the story goes, the *Serpent* upended the first couple's idyllic habitat and, ever since, human beings have been wary of slithering fork-tongued creatures. Shortly afterwards, their social network expanded to include their two sons, Cain and Abel. Once again, a stealthy intruder came calling disguised as the *Grim Reaper*, who egged on Cain to murder his brother in cold blood.

According to the traditional Judeo-Christian account, following the *Great Flood* that destroyed the Earth, the survivors' descendants *"had one language and a common speech"* and organised themselves into a homogeneous network. Subsequently, they conspired to *"build a city, with a tower that reaches to the heavens."* Again, the story did not end well. At the *Tower of Babel*, their language became confused and they were scattered over the face of the Earth.

Humanity's early attempts at socialising *and* networking thus culminated in a crippling strikeout after a dismal batting performance. Starting with the geometric sequence 2^0 *(Home Alone or network-challenged Adam)* to 2^1 in the *Garden of Eden,* to 2^2 outside the perimeter of *Eden*, to 2^n at *Babel*, these origin stories heralded *DECEPTION, DEATH* and *DIVISION*, respectively into human affairs. Since then, the world's population has ballooned to $2^{32.85}$, or 7.7 billion (need proof that the devil is in the decimals? Well, $2^{32.5}$ = 6.1 billion and 2^{33} = 8.6 billion), as at August 2019.

During the intervening period, the human spirit has remained indefatigable, subconsciously seeking to retrace its steps back to *Babel*, although *Eden* remains out of bounds. Incidentally, by virtue of technological innovation, it seems that artificial intelligence (AI) is at the cusp of enabling instantaneous, real-time language translation, while the largest social networks in history are being stitched together.

Two questions come to mind. Technically, what is a social network, and why are we so enamoured of human connectivity? Second, if minuscule networks conjured the aforementioned disasters, what types of creepy-crawlies might be prowling billions-strong digital networks in the 21st century?

The term "social network" is a standard construct used to study the interactions between individuals, groups, organisations, and communities. In societies where individual agency confers fundamental human rights, the notion of each citizen being equivalent to a *network node* is an extremely powerful concept. In such a scenario, a *network node* represents a connection point within a distributed network that can store, create, receive or send information, which is a perfect characterisation of the human need to communicate.

Now, assume that every individual within a society knows 100 independent people. It therefore implies that, theoretically, each person or *network node* is one step removed from a connection to 10,000 other people, and so on. This rolling cascade typifies the network effect, and explains why Facebook (or its Chinese equivalent) is so unbelievably powerful and dominant.

Conventional wisdom suggests that new technologies foster upsides and downsides. While optimists tout net positive outcomes, naysayers often warn about the end of civilisation as we know it. Despite numerous benefits, social media platforms have been blamed for an increase in attention deficit hyperactivity disorders, low self-esteem, depression, *anti-social* personality disorders, cyberbullying, trolling, extortion, suicides, erosion of privacy, spread of false information, and the rise of a global network of hate.

Furthermore, the ludicrous notion that social media services are *free* flies in the face of the axiom that *"there's no free lunch."* By trading personal data for a *free* service, subscribers should be aware that their online posts *"cannot be entirely deleted,"* which means that records of indiscretions remain in purgatory.

Even more pernicious is the fact that troves of subscribers' data are subjected to algorithmic AI processing. Typically unregulated, generated outputs are often sold to marketing companies and prospective employers, and are being used to manipulate voters' intentions. Also, surveillance and non-surveillance states alike are deploying facial-recognition software without seeking citizens' consent. And with deepfake voice and video, soon we might not be able to distinguish the authentic from the unreal. On this evidence, what exactly does the future portend?

If *"what has been will be again,"* it is plausible that the spirit of a malevolent, winged, fire-belching mythical *DRAGON* - an amalgam of our worst nightmares and pathologies - has already infiltrated the atmosphere and is now stalking cyberspace, including the deep recesses of the so-called *Dark Web*.

Real or imagined, memories of old demons die hard.

CHAPTER 20

Waterloo

From the perspective of a non-American, who has absolutely no skin in the game, I still experience mental whiplash whenever I hear an American politician offer "thoughts and prayers" after a mass shooting in the country. However, following the recent spate of mindless mayhem, I did a double-take when a hyper-partisan *National Rifle Association*-affiliated talking head uttered the phrase *"I feel your pain"* on television. Involuntarily, I sputtered, *"No, you don't."*

The range of issues dividing conservatives and progressives in the world's most dynamic liberal democracy keeps growing. From social arguments about abortion, sanctity of marriage, multiculturalism, and religion to disagreements over tax rates, social security, immigration, and globalisation, the chasm is widening. Politics has become so tribal and bifurcated that compromise is now a filthy word. Paradoxically, social networks that were supposedly designed to unite people have instead spawned hermetically-sealed echo chambers of mutual incomprehension. The fount of public opinion is so badly poisoned that both sides offhandedly reject the other's viewpoints in a bid to affirm their fidelity and ideological purity.

Take climate change. Let us concede that this is a fiendishly complex issue that nevertheless demands the urgent attention of the world's largest economies and polluters, principally China and the US. Proponents in the US will rightly point to science-based evidence for global warming, primarily caused by greenhouse gas emissions. On the other side of the divide are right-wingers, dubbed "anti-science and anti-expert," who oppose government regulations, dispute environmental claims, and revel in being called hoaxers. Even the *Paris Agreement,* which aims to limit our planet's long-term average temperature increase relative to pre-industrial levels, is dismissed as a global ploy by leftists against US interests.

If there is no consensus on climate change, could there however be some common ground concerning the spectre of global water shortages in the coming decades? Again, sceptics are liable to revive the debunked theory linking food scarcity to population growth. Besides, water scarcity sounds like someone else's problem, the type mostly faced by poor developing countries. But, is it?

Among our most essential physiological needs, *air, food* and *water* are topmost. Air is abundant and envelopes us, but it is highly vulnerable to industrial and energy pollution. Food and water are sometimes in short supply around the world, especially in drought-prone areas. But of the three, water has suddenly risen to the summit of global consciousness, possibly because it has no obvious substitute. Without water, human beings simply cannot survive. And as the world's population grows, so does the demand for water, even if this is only half the story.

Ominously, scientists believe that climate change has aggravated spells of severe drought, land degradation and desertification. It would therefore not be an overstatement that a global water crisis could become the greatest existential peril confronting hundreds of millions of people, and the problem could be about to get worse.

To better appreciate the gravity of the situation, hydrologists are deploying satellite technology to measure the world's water reserves, taking account of groundwater, rivers, rainfall, and other sources. Current statistics are quite sobering and long-term projections are equally gloomy. 70% of the most highly water-stressed countries in the world are in the Middle East and the northern reaches of Africa. And, unsurprisingly, this arid and perpetually volatile area is where competition over water resources is greatest. Desalination could be part of the mix of possible solutions, but it is very expensive and also raises the level of environmental concerns. If parts of India and Brazil are included, about a quarter of the world's population is under serious threat from droughts and water shortages.

A recent article went as far as suggesting that *"the next world war is going to be fought not over oil or mineral wealth, but over water."* Even if this statement is somewhat over the top, what may focus attention everywhere is the ongoing waves of human migration. Take Nigeria, where the world's attention has been on *Boko Haram*, an indigenous Islamic terrorist group. But, simultaneously, regional herdsmen from across West Africa, retreating from encroaching desertification, have invaded and are literally overrunning southern Nigeria. Internal flash points are going off by the day.

Meanwhile, nativists and xenophobes in richer countries could soon glimpse their waterloo when confronted by the exodus of economic migrants and climate-change refugees from the southern hemisphere. This is a script that could develop this century if the perfect storm of extreme weather, economic deprivation, internal strife, high population growth in the poorest countries, chronic food shortages, and, crucially, lack of access to potable water, unfolds. In the same ballpark as climate change, water poverty demands an immediate and coordinated global response.

Logically, *conservatives* should support water conservation and other resource efficiency initiatives, but bizarrely, the opposite is true. In short order, *"I feel your 'thirst'"*, a semantically imprecise but hypocritical refrain, may soon fill the airwaves. To be clear, thirst, like pain, has no ideology.

As ideological foes weigh the cost of intransigence, might the scramble for water inadvertently wash away some of the antipathy between bleeding-heart liberals and dyed-in-the-wool conservatives? Let's drink to that, but don't hold your breath.

CHAPTER 21

Reform, Not

There are buzzwords and then there are mega buzzwords. In business, when nudged into making an elevator pitch, white-collar executives might rehash their corporate *strategy*. In the public sector, politicians and policymakers, with very little prompting, tend to bang on about *reform*. Doubtless, *strategy* and *reform* are credible word cloud favourites in a media age clogged with widgets that spew out useful metadata and superfluous statistics, more of the latter.

Because the future is unknowable and it is in human nature to dream and to pursue new ideas and opportunities, our desire for change is insatiable. *Change* is another mega buzzword that means different things to different people. In a corporate or public context, the perennial challenge is how to foster a shared change agenda, with the ultimate aim of improving people's economic and social well-being. The classical change mechanisms are either top-down or bottom-up, but it is usually more nuanced than that.

In a *business* setting, the impetus for change can range from limited to non-existent if there is one dominant player, more so if the entity is a monopoly. Where competition exists, typically companies vie for market share and seek to maximise shareholder value by implementing diverse strategies. To improve the odds of achieving its objectives, an organisation's top management crafts a strategic plan, in turn endorsed by a majority of stakeholders. Faced with grave external threats, a company's survival may sometimes demand radical overhaul, rather than simple tweaks, through massive restructuring, disruptive innovation or creative destruction.

In the *public* sphere, societies organised in a rigid hierarchy and helmed by a monarch or autocrat are usually resistant to change. Because the primary goal of the leader is survival, rather than the citizens' best interests, every other consideration is secondary. History has shown that when opposing views are stifled, freedom is curtailed, and agitators are locked up, such situations can precipitate an extreme reaction such as a people's revolution. In pluralistic societies, where political parties compete for power, the clamour for reform can be relentless.

From time immemorial, politicians fall over each other with myriad promises about how to *"rectify or improve what is wrong, to make things better."* In the best or worst of times, this can be a tall order for either bravehearts or charlatans pursuing public office. To hedge their bets, politicians who position themselves as change candidates often use it as a ploy to discredit establishment rivals or to make a case for a generational transfer of power.

Typically, politicians publish campaign manifestos that are then boiled down to outlandish pledges on the stump. More often than not, the outcomes fall short in practice, which then results in recriminations. Without making excuses for public office-seekers, when a politician creates a campaign sound bite, it stems from a set of assumptions. Assumptions are precisely that, and they depend on unpredictable events and how multitudes of people will behave in the future. Therefore, when a campaign promise is translated into official policy, which is when reality bumps against the fine prints of a manifesto, and reform programmes might start to unravel.

Mind you, it is important to remember that political and socio-economic reform is ultimately about people; essentially, its purpose is to improve *"living standards and the quality of life."* At the national level, the most critical reforms tend to impact macroeconomic policy, public finance, financial markets, and public infrastructure. Structural reforms cover areas such as the civil service, tax and regulatory policy, labour markets, and the welfare state.

While monarchs, despots or elected leaders can be dislodged from office, an entrenched civil service is constant and immovable, and could be the most difficult to reform. Manifestly, a bloated, inefficient, and possibly corrupt bureaucracy often spells the death knell of the most well-intentioned policy reforms.

Back to the retail end, the litmus test of any reform agenda is its positive impact on constituents' lives. But, here's a surprising and very insightful twist. However broadly reform programmes are defined, eventually they circle back to the individual. And for reforms to gain traction and succeed, the governed have two primary responsibilities. First, when leaders, legislators, public officials, and the like fail to perform, the people have the collective civic responsibility to speak truth to power. Of course, it is infinitely much easier to do so in a free society. Under an autocracy, dissidents risk being locked up or killed. But, even in such dire circumstances, being passive and complicit is hardly a good strategy for evicting an unyielding tyrant.

Second, as economic agents, every one of us has the responsibility to keep boosting our productivity through skills development, lifelong learning, and by adapting to new tools. By squeezing more out of available resources, and workers imbibing a strong work ethic, government reforms have a fighting chance of bearing fruits, thereby raising living standards. Inevitably, there will be winners and losers, requiring social cohesion measures to redress imbalances.

In the final analysis, not reforming implies stagnation, maybe a slide into precipitous decline. Patently, reform is not the sole responsibility of other people - *them*. By renewing the mind and spirit, every individual has the obligation to steer the world away from retrogression or, perish the thought, anarchy.

CHAPTER 22

Hand-Me-Down

Nostalgia is a double-edged device that can flood the mind with positive memories, but sometimes could be tinged with regret. Recently, I came across a newspaper article titled *"The Appliances That Just Go On And On."* The story featured reminiscences by respondents waxing lyrical about their time-defying domestic gadgets, several of which had traversed two generations, and others waxing indignant about more modern acquisitions.

The standout narrative recounted *Hoover* fridges that were installed by English councils in the mid-1950s. A woman's mother-in-law moved into one of those council houses in Northumberland in 1956, and guess what? The fridge is still chugging along. A couple bought the same brand, but a different model, 46 years ago and, apart from frequent defrosting, they've chosen not to replace it. Other *Hall of Fame* brands from that era include *Electrolux, Kenwood, Moulinex* and *Swan,* spanning cookers, washing machines, blenders, toasters, and humble kettles.

The resonance of these anecdotes is unmistakable because of my parallel experience. Although I cannot remember the brand, we had an imposing, slightly off-kilter refrigerator in my youth that reminded me of the *Leaning Tower of Pisa*. Purchased in the 1950s, this appliance outlasted flashier, newer versions procured two decades later. By the late 1980s, the old reliable would intermittently create a racket by emitting a guttural sound, as though clearing up its vocal pipes. Eventually, my father decided to retire it to our country home, whereupon the story trailed off. Also imprinted in my memory was our sturdy cooker built like a *Chieftain* battle tank, as well as my mother's *Kenwood* food processor that never seemed to quit.

Another searing tale from that period was of a relative whose father had died, and left him possibly his most prized possession - his bicycle. By then, the son had travelled abroad, started his own family, and risen to become a university professor. On a visit to his home town, he came upon his inheritance and, to his horror, discovered that someone had vandalised his father's bicycle. Uncharacteristically, he hit the roof. After calming down, he ensured that the bike was repaired and restored to mint condition, before carting it away.

Laugh if you will, but the care exhibited by the professor towards a lowly bicycle is comparable to the devotion displayed by individuals who inherit priceless Swiss watches, such as *Patek Philippe, Rolex,* and equivalent brands. Painstakingly hand-crafted by skilled artisans, these watches and similar family heirlooms were built to last, and last, and last.

From a different perspective, I have sometimes pondered the changes that have occurred within nuclear families going back in time, when couples had as many as four to six children. As the third of four myself, I recall my father taking me to his tailor periodically when I had the privilege of selecting a batch of custom-made clothes - from suits to shirts and trousers. In those days, this practice was not unusual. Nevertheless, it was commonplace for children, irrespective of social class, to wear *hand-me-down* clothes and shoes from older siblings and cousins. Don't snigger. That was just the way it was, when I would contend that consumer products were markedly more hard-wearing or durable.

Then, suddenly, everything seemed to change. The dizzying rise of consumerism could be attributed to a range of factors. Here are some suggestions. First, under domestic economic pressure, the US government decided in 1971 to decouple the dollar from the international gold standard, thus ending the convertibility that had existed since the end of WW2. This led to freely floating currencies, and volatility. Second, the Organisation of Petroleum Exporting Countries (OPEC) sent shock waves through the global economy by spiking the price of crude oil, in response to the US Middle East policy.

Consequently, economic stagflation ensued throughout the 1970s, causing double-digit inflation, high unemployment rates and slowing economies. Simultaneously, the world's population had risen from less than 2.5 billion in the mid-1940s to about 4.0 billion by 1975. It is plausible that the liberal economic model adapted to changing demographics and dire economic circumstances by mass-producing affordable goods for an exploding consumer market.

Therefore, in place of the old-fashioned frugal mindset, a new throwaway culture was born. Perhaps the greatest irony was that the counter-cultural, seemingly anti-materialistic, baby-boomer generation that came of age in the 1960s then presided over the most egregious exploitation of our planet's natural resources in history. Furthermore, by having fewer children, indulgent boomers orchestrated the nurturing of self-centred, sometimes narcissistic, children and grandchildren with a monumental sense of entitlement. Aided and abetted by wily marketing companies, advertisers promoted the idea that nothing was quite good enough, by coaxing people into worshipping the new and faddish.

In time, industrialised nations proceeded to manufacture cheaper products, with relatively short life cycles, which kept their economies ticking over. As their landfills and incinerators overflowed, a perverse version of *hand-me-down* between rich and poor countries took root. Before long, waste products of all shapes and sizes - second-hand cars, home appliances, hazardous electronic goods, and sundry items - were being shipped to the world's most impoverished consumers, whose recycling savvy is marginal at best. The hypocrisy underlying this flagrant practice has never been addressed.

And, incredibly, we all wonder why the global ecosystem is straining under the weight of runaway pollution and degradation. First, look in the mirror.

CHAPTER 23

Plastics Everywhere

Dustin Hoffman's breakout film role as Benjamin Braddock in the 1967 movie *The Graduate* featured a young man fresh out of college. During a *tête-à-tête with* a family friend, Mr. Mcguire, Benjamin received a one-word career advice: *"Plastics."* For emphasis, Mcguire repeated, *"There's a great future in plastics. Think about it. Will you think about it?"*

Sure enough, in the aftermath of this fictional exchange, many *S.T.E.M. (Science, Technology, Engineering and Mathematics)* undergraduates, and graduate students, followed Mr. Mcguire's counsel by studying polymer science, chemical engineering, plastics technology, and related courses. Indeed, there was strong evidence that the so-called petro-plastics industry boomed in subsequent decades.

More than half a century later, were the avatar of Mcguire to offer a similar career tip, what would it be? In one word, probably: *"Data."* And it does seem as if many of today's Benjamin Braddocks are opting for careers in fields like computer engineering, data science and cybersecurity. In the past decade, the amount of data generated worldwide has exploded, thus jump-starting the so-called *Big Data Mining and Analytics* revolution. Without question, the data economy is reshaping all aspects of our lives. For instance, the volume of data produced annually between 2010 and 2019 increased twentyfold to about 40 zettabytes (40 X 10^{21} bytes!). With the advent of 5G communications networks and *Internet-of-Things*, this figure is expected to continue its steep ascent.

Connecting the dots from plastics to data, however spurious, underscores the pervasive nature of both. The quantum of structured data, residing in companies' data warehouses and data marts, as well as in *cloud* storage, in addition to an avalanche of unstructured data created on social media platforms and across the Internet, can only be imagined. Overwhelmed by 24-hour news cycles and, with search engines enabling instantaneous access to unlimited gobs of knowledge assets, the sense of information overload is palpable, where once there was scarcity.

However, unlike *1s* and *0s* abstractions that make up data bits and bytes, plastic is a tangible, organic material. Thanks to Mr. Mcguire and other boosters of the powerful petrochemical industry, it seems as though the world has been overrun by plastic products. Producers and governments everywhere are culpable, and the conspiracy of silence about the environmental ramifications has been deafening.

So, how did we arrive at this juncture? Synthetic plastic was invented in the US about 112 years ago, but it was the discovery of nylon, a purely synthetic fibre, in 1939 that transformed the polymer industry. Plastics are organic polymers produced from petrochemical compounds, as well as from natural substances like corn and cotton. To provide some perspective, before plastics became ubiquitous, manufacturers and fabricators utilised substrates such as wood, metal, glass, ceramic and stone. Relative to the physical properties of these materials, plastic is not only low-cost but water-resistant, malleable and highly mouldable, making it the first and sometimes the only choice for casting many familiar products.

It is important to acknowledge the immense benefits that plastics have contributed to economies globally. Aside from large-scale applications in industries as diverse as automotive and construction, plastics are so versatile that nowadays they show up just about everywhere - in healthcare, agriculture, electronics, toys and sporting goods. In addition, plastic exists in everyday products such as chewing gum, bottle caps and packaging. Without exaggeration, it is difficult to imagine the retail industry devoid of food wrappers and plastic grocery bags. Indeed, while packaging represents as much as a third of plastic use in industrialised economies, the figure is over 40% in India and many developing countries.

On the downside, the more dependent we have become on plastics, accentuated by our mobile lifestyles, so have environmental concerns grown, due to the slow decomposition rates of plastic products. It is estimated that it takes between 50 and 500 years for items like plastic cups, cigarette butt filters, and disposable nappies to fully degrade. Concerned or not, there has been no escaping the horrific images splashed on television screens of dead marine creatures along seafronts, shown with plastic fibres and fragments in their digestive tracts.

To my mind, it would take someone with a strong stomach not to retch or turn away in disgust.

Despite the best intentions, recycling efforts have failed to curb the intensifying plastic pollution. Unlike metallic objects, products with multiple plastic parts can be very difficult to sort by resin type using automated processes, meaning that the effort is usually labour-intensive and expensive. Where the technology exists, thermoplastics can be melted and re-used. However, in poorer countries, open-air burning of plastic wastes releases toxic, sometimes carcinogenic, fumes into the atmosphere. But, more than likely, the bulk of such wastes ends up in waterways and ocean basins.

In an age when we tend to believe that technology can solve most problems, unfortunately no commercially-viable substitute has been found for plastic. And, for all our sakes, it is imperative that the general public is educated about the misconception about the efficacy of bioplastics and bio-degradable plastic. Bioplastics are made from renewable materials like corn; however, bioplastics represent just about 0.2% of the total global production of non-renewable alternatives. Contrary to expectations, 'bio-degradable' in fact implies partial decomposition; therefore, tossing a bio-degradable product into the sea is almost as problematic for marine life as ordinary plastic. Significantly, the production of plastics that can degrade through exposure to sunlight, water, bacteria or special enzymes is limited, due to relatively high costs.

So, whither the future of plastics? Apparently, since we cannot wish plastics away, the most authoritative suggestion by experts is that we produce and use less of the materials. More specifically, they recommend a ban on single-use plastic products like shopping bags, plastic bottles, stirrers and straws. Since a re-use, and recycle, policy cannot be unilaterally enforced, some governments have imposed, for example, a tax on grocery bags to modulate consumers' behaviour.

If Mr. Mcguire could have envisioned the unintended consequences of his advice to young Benjamin Braddock, would he perhaps have been more circumspect? The answer is bobbing on the waterfront.

CHAPTER 24

Crossroads

Move fast but try not to move faster than the speed of thought, especially if you are approaching a crossroads. Semantically, crossroads is a word than hides its singularity under the guise of plurality. A crossroads is, in fact, the *intersection* of two or more roads that also signifies a crucial decision point.

In November 1999, Jack Welch was named the *Manager of the Century* by *Fortune* magazine, the most prestigious business publication in the US. Welch had been the chief executive officer (CEO) of General Electric Company (GE) since 1980, and his retirement was imminent. He was nicknamed *Neutron Jack* for his take-no-prisoners management style and, over time, GE was voted the world's most admired business organisation. Under his leadership,

GE's market capitalisation rose 4,000%, rising to $410 billion in 2001.

Founded in 1892, this industrial and financial conglomerate's DNA had been infused with the innovative genius of Thomas Edison, widely acknowledged as one of the greatest inventors who ever lived. Between Edison and Welch, only ten other men had been privileged to steer GE's storied legacy. By 2001, literally and figuratively, the company was approaching possibly the most consequential crossroads in its history. But, riding the waves of spectacular success, no one at GE, including Jack Welch, could have anticipated what was ahead.

Before revisiting GE, let me touch on a brief, if subjective, analysis of the nature of crossroads. Assume a man is journeying from the south-west. On reaching a crossroads, the options are to proceed in a north-east direction, turn south-east or move north-west. This is the classic X configuration. Faced with these options, let us agree that the subject cannot turn back in the direction he came from nor can he choose to remain motionless at the junction. Furthermore, the subject cannot allege that the highway was cloaked in pitch darkness such that he drove straight on, oblivious of the intersection.

Lastly, since the technology is yet to be perfected, he also cannot claim to have been riding in an autonomous vehicle with a mind of its own.

Left with three valid options, the path to a decision seems clearer but no less fraught with peril. If the south-west road was broad and the trip hitch-free, his natural inclination might be to proceed north-east. By failing to notice other vehicles at the intersection, an overconfident or inattentive driver could easily be side-swiped into a tailspin. On the other hand, a tortuous approach journey along a narrow and bumpy road might elicit more caution. From the foregoing, access to pertinent information is crucial in deciding whether to turn south-east or north-west. But, however unimpeachable the quality of information at-hand, the future is usually a black box.

In 2001, Jack Welch was a rock star CEO who, presciently, had declared in 1991 that his succession plan was the most important challenge ahead of him. He would later identify three internal candidates who were made to jump through hoops before he hand-picked his successor, Jeffrey Immelt. Compared to Welch, who was a hard-nosed engineer with a Ph.D., Immelt was a relatively genteel Harvard MBA graduate. The also-rans, both excellent executives in a company renowned for developing top-notch leaders, quietly left GE, leaving the field open to the incoming boss. On his part, Welch also quit the GE board with a $417 million retirement package, the largest ever in US corporate history.

Just four days after Immelt took the reins at GE, *9/11* happened like a bolt out of the blue. As one of the world's largest manufacturers of commercial aircraft engines, the terrorist attacks, which saw planes being flown into New York City's *Twin Towers,* was the equivalent of a sucker punch to GE's solar plexus. Also, in the shadow of the dot-com crash and the Enron scandal, the surviving tyros of the burgeoning digital age threw down the gauntlet and would soon transform and reshape the old industrial economy.

While contending with an identity crisis, and before GE could regain its balance, the worst financial crisis since the *Great Depression* struck in 2008. Subsequently, GE Capital, which at its peak had contributed as much as 60% to GE's profitability, became embroiled in a financial maelstrom. Along with other divested subsidiaries like NBC Universal, GE Plastics and GE Appliances, most of the assets of GE Capital were subsequently sold off by Immelt. Consistently underperforming the markets during his reign, GE's market value plummeted by $150 billion or 37%. Inevitably, investors lost patience with Immelt in 2017, who effectively left behind a complex but hollowed-out shell of the *"house that Jack built."*

On the heels of tough financial reforms, GE had no choice but to return to its industrial roots. Like empires before it, search engines threw up captions along the lines of *"The Rise and Fall of GE"* and *"Who is Responsible for the Mess at GE?"* Since Immelt's departure, GE has had two CEOs in the space of two years. The incumbent CEO, Lawrence Culp Jr., replaced John Flannery, whose tenure was marked by turmoil and a further decline in the company's fortunes.

GE's current outlook is rather grim, causing many to question whether the company would ever regain its lustre. Of course, nothing lasts for ever and no organisation has the right to perpetual success. In essence, crossroads can be benign when all the stars are perfectly aligned, while a wrong move could prove irredeemably fatal.

Significantly, Culp was the first outsider to run GE in its 128-year history. With the benefit of hindsight, perhaps an outsider, a disruptor and mould-breaker was precisely who should have succeeded Welch back in 2001. Expectedly, expert analysts and armchair critics alike have had a field day second-guessing Immelt's tenure, as well as the logic of GE's acquisitive business model.

Was it possible that Jack Welch was, indeed, a singularly gifted CEO who functioned at the speed of thought whereas Jeff Immelt could not? Presumably, Immelt stuck to the familiar and insular *GE Way*, kept glancing in the rear-view mirror and missed vital warning signs.

CHAPTER 25

Out of Sight

How tiny is tiny? Or how thin is thin? A pharaoh ant or a strand of hair, perhaps? Sounds like a specious response to a silly quiz. In fact, human cognition allows us to perceive nature at, and beyond, eye-level resolution while innate curiosity leads us to explore our environment in all its complexity. Unprompted, we are constantly seeking to make sense of our place in a universe containing objects both great and small.

In Jonathan Swift's *Gulliver's Travels,* we are treated to a satire featuring several voyages undertaken by Lemuel Gulliver. On his first trip, he was shipwrecked and held prisoner on the island of *Lilliput*, inhabited by a race of tiny, half-foot tall people. With more than a ten-fold height advantage,

Gulliver had to be extremely nimble around the *Lilliputians* to avoid harming them. Bizarrely, they possessed a sense of self-importance that belied their small size, starkly demonstrated when the *Lilliputians'* army corps paraded around and between Gulliver's legs. On returning home, Gulliver next visited the *Brobingnagians*, a race of giants, on average about twelve times taller than Gulliver. While his new hosts were more hospitable than the *Lilliputians*, he never felt comfortable or safe amongst them, beside the fact that the *Brobingnagians* treated him like an exhibit in a freak show.

The political undertones in *Gulliver's Travels* are unmistakable, but do not subsume the simple inference that size is relative. Outside a customary frame of reference, thinkers often resort to thought experiments to speculate about worlds unseen, while well-kitted researchers have been able to probe natural phenomena more objectively. In due course, two amazing instruments - the periscope and microscope - magnified and forever changed our perception of the physical world.

While the study of the universe is largely the domain of astronomers and cosmologists who deploy relatively expensive instrumentation, the study of small organisms and objects is comparatively within reach. Dating back to the early 17th century, the invention of the compound microscope (which combines an objective lens with a viewing eyepiece) has evolved to modern scanning probe microscopes with unprecedented capabilities.

Welcome to the world of nanoscience and nanotechnology - the study and manipulation of objects at the atomic and sub-molecular scale, in the order of a nanometre (10^{-9} metre). So, in relative terms, how wide is a nanometre? A spherical object with a diameter of one nanometre is comparable in size to a football, as a football is to planet Earth!

With the invention of the scanning tunnelling microscope almost four decades ago, it became possible to manipulate sub-molecular particles at that level of resolution for the fabrication of macroscale products. Since the early years, nanotechnology has found applications in diverse industries, including energy, manufacturing, agriculture, pharmaceuticals, cosmetics, sports, transportation, electronics, and healthcare.

Essentially, there are two methodologies employed in nanotechnology. First, there is the *bottom-up* approach, whereby nanomaterials and nanodevices are assembled from the ground up at the molecular level. By contrast, the *top-down* mode of microfabrication begins on a larger scale without molecular control. So far, possibly the greatest advances have emerged in the commercial nanoelectronic semiconductor sector, which underpins the high-technology industry.

To be clear, no one is suggesting that people should stop hankering after smartphone upgrades. However, due to an intuitive sense of self-preservation, healthcare probably occupies a special perch in our consciousness. As an emerging discipline, nanomedicine explores the impact of nanotechnology on medical interventions such as diagnostics, drug delivery, blood purification, tissue engineering, as well as the fabrication of bio-sensors and bio-nanodevices.

To all those who look forward to the day when *"going under the knife"* will be severely curtailed or obsolete, nanomedicine would be a godsend. This new dawn could presumably empower medical personnel to, in situ, repair damaged tissue, remove toxins and pathogens from blood, deliver drug nanoparticles to targeted sites, and use biological nanomachines to weld arteries. As nanomedicine matures and becomes more widely accessible, minimally invasive surgery will become a game-changing reality.

If you are dismayed by the idea of autonomous nanomachines performing surgeries, the good news is that microsurgery would most likely remain under the control of human surgeons. When it comes to matters of life and death, most people would rather leave decision-making and crucial judgments in the hands of trained doctors instead of artificial intelligence-enabled (AI) robots. *Out of sight* medical procedures should not necessarily translate into the total abdication of human responsibility.

Nanotechnology, like space exploration, is opening up a new frontier that is pointing the way to a brave new world where archetypes of *Lilliputians* and *Brobingnagians* will continue to challenge our imagination.

CHAPTER 26

Tainted Glass

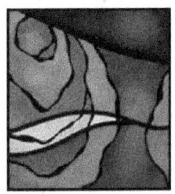

Ignorance can be bliss but, sometimes and depending on the circumstances, ignorance could be debilitating. Earlier this year, a television documentary explored the rise of anti-Semitism in Europe. Survey results revealed that a third of respondents in seven countries were unaware of the death camps strewn across German-occupied Europe three-quarters of a century ago. In the US, they discovered that two-thirds of American students were clueless about the *Holocaust* perpetrated by the Nazis.

Recoiling from WW2 crimes against humanity, well-meaning people everywhere periodically echoed the mantra *"Never Again."* Yet, unconscionably, we've since had attempted genocide in Cambodia and Rwanda. For history not to keep repeating itself, it raises the question of how well this all-important subject is being taught in schools. Parsing that statement, it may be more pertinent to ask why certain fields of study are not mandatory in junior and high school education. For instance, to convey the full horror of not only fascism but other variants of totalitarianism, it would be helpful if students are exposed to the Communist ideology, and learn why tens of millions perished in Soviet gulags and Chinese labour camps.

Even when history is officially sanctioned, off and on it is beamed through tainted glass. A case in point is the Japanese establishment. As an occupying force in China and Korea before and during WW2, Japanese textbooks have continuously, and unapologetically, played down the transgressions of the Imperial Japanese Army. Decades on, the country's distorted version of history has soured diplomatic relations and raised tensions with its neighbours.

Unfortunately for state actors, the Internet as a platform has completely transformed how information is generated and consumed. Worldwide, malicious intrusion by trolls and cyberterrorists has grown unbounded but, ironically, nations that undermine cybersecurity are equally susceptible to hacking. Despite this, the volume, variety and velocity of data traffic in cyberspace is increasing exponentially, to such an extent that even repressive governments struggle to retain control.

State censorship is not a new phenomenon. Before the invention of the printing press in the 15th century, church authorities had a virtual lock on the dissemination of information. The religious manuscripts in circulation, mostly hand-copied by monks, were ultimately swamped by secular books that would shape public opinion in unimaginable ways. With the genie out of the bottle, the ability of power centres to control the creation and propagation of information became ever more difficult. Two other inflection points coincided with the invention of the radio and television, both of which authorities feared would facilitate the spread of false information.

Over time, the perceived threats posed by the printing press, radio and television were no less disorienting than those that we are experiencing today. All the anxiety about fake news and alternative facts feed into the narrative espoused by illiberal politicians and populists who seek to sow dissonance and disunity. While grown-ups are no less vulnerable, the concern persists about the accuracy of what highly impressionable youngsters are being exposed to online and offline. In light of the deluge of contradictory and ideologically-tainted information being trafficked on news channels and social media platforms, it is easy to be pessimistic about the impact this must be having globally. Is such despair warranted? Yes and No.

Yes, because non-democratic forces and unscrupulous politicians will not relent from promoting a refracted worldview, as long as it boosts their hold on power. In democratic circles, sadly it seems as though there are few adults left in politics. At a time when democratic institutions and liberal principles are under attack, leaders with a poor grasp of history, and who dismiss the minutiae of statecraft, are conducting governance and diplomacy by *Twitter!* Where cool heads are needed, those who should know better lie routinely and matter-of-factly, while fuelling malign conspiracy theories.

In bygone years, when *viral* was a simple biological term, such (mis)behaviour would have been ridiculed and marginalised by raised voices from both sides of the political divide. These days, when unfiltered posts can be shared instantly by billions, the risk of misunderstanding and misinterpretation is sky high. For all our sakes, we must hope that hair-trigger miscalculations do not expose us all to maximum peril in a world brimming with nuclear warheads.

No, because if we survive the aforementioned apocalyptic scenario, order might eventually supplant the current chaos. Disinformation, in concert with oversaturation, is a serious problem; however, this also provides an opportunity for innovators. That is part of the genius of free societies whereby new markets emerge under the most unlikely circumstances. Soon, we should expect a market for accurate or more objective information to emerge, once a critical mass decides to seek refuge from the ongoing assault on common sense.

From school textbooks to news sources, wily entrepreneurs will most likely launch trusted, well-researched, and expertly curated platforms that would eventually gain broad recognition. That may not completely dislodge dangerous holdouts, such as *Holocaust* deniers, hate-mongers and pernicious *YouTube* polemicists, from trying to poison the well. In the event, it would be down to individuals to discern truth from fiction. Hopefully, the future will inspire a less sullied, more transcendent mindset in people that will help to separate the wheat from shiploads of information chaff.

CHAPTER 27

Cuckoo's Nest

Every human being possesses one or more talents that vary across a broad spectrum. Deploying our primary senses, we interface with the world through our vision, auditory perception, touch, and other faculties. But while the majority of people perceive nature simply and unvarnished, there are outliers who instinctively search for patterns with their eyes either open or wide shut, indicative of how their brains are wired. Using symbols, logic and pure imagination, gifted mathematicians have the capacity to study the shape and motion of physical objects, and to delineate space in abstraction. As far as the average person is concerned, these brainiacs might as well exist in a parallel universe.

Often when we encounter creative types, such as

musicians, fine artists, writers, and prodigious number-crunchers, their non-conventional character traits tend to mark them out as slightly *cuckoo*, which is not a term of endearment. In this rarefied world, mathematics geeks are a special breed who have provided the underpinning for scientific enquiry in physics, chemistry, engineering, astronomy, and many other fields of study.

Once in a while, even mathematicians encounter problems to which there are no known solutions. One of such uncanny puzzles challenged the best minds in Ancient Greece. For those who absolutely detested geometry as students, the next statement might bring back spastic memories, but try to hang on. *"Given a circle, the challenge is to construct - using only a straight-edge and compass - a square equal in area to that circle."* Well, Greek geometers tried and tried, as did others subsequently, but no one succeeded. *Just when someone thought that the puzzle had been resolved, it was discovered that their solution was only an approximation.*

Not until the 19th century was it definitively proved that the problem could not be solved in a finite number of steps. Thereafter, the phrase *"squaring the circle"* entered our vocabulary to describe the futility of attempting the impossible.

Staying with the theme of elusive puzzles, the first time I watched the movie *One Flew Over The Cuckoo's Nest (OFOTCN)*, I was too young to fully grasp the plot lines. Coming of age during my mathematics-obsessed head-in-the-clouds years, the film provided my first glimpse inside an asylum. Though creepy, my experience was amplified by Jack Nicholson's stunning performance as *Randle McMurphy*. Edgy and disturbing in parts, the cast of loonies included outstanding actors like Danny DeVito, Christopher Lloyd and Brad Dourif. Decades later, when I viewed *OFOTCN* the second time, I finally understood why *McMurphy's* ploy mirrored a doomed attempt to *square the circle.*

Briefly, *Randle McMurphy* was a criminal who had been convicted for rape, assault and battery. Even though he was not mentally ill, *McMurphy* was momentarily transferred from a regular prison to a mental hospital. There, he encountered certified patients under the stern supervision of autocratic *Nurse Ratched,* brilliantly portrayed by Louise Fletcher. Despite the strict and austere environment, *McMurphy* preferred spending the rest of his sentence there rather than return to the hard labour regime at the prison. With the passage of time, his devious personality permeated the institution, often bumping against *Nurse Ratched's* authority.

In time, *McMurphy* became aware that his sentencing judge had ruled that the time he spent in the asylum would not defray or reduce the length of his original sentence. Therefore, *McMurphy* faced the risk of being trapped in his new abode indefinitely. Realising that his scheme had failed, he began to plot his escape. Having won several skirmishes, ultimately he lost the war when he was apprehended, lobotomised, and returned to the mental institution in a vegetative state. *Just when McMurphy thought that he had outmanoeuvred everybody, he discovered that the system had him in a vice-like grip all along.*

Another inadvertent example of a *cuckoo* attempting to *square the circle* is illustrated by the experience of a pilot in the classic novel *Catch-22*. Like *OFOTCN,* there is a large dose of macabre humour at the heart of this story. Captain *John Yossarian* was a US air force bombardier stationed on an island off the coast of Italy during WW2. The tale depicts the absurdity of war as, progressively, *Yossarian's* antipathy towards his commanders actually grew worse than his fear of Germans. Feeling that his side was *"out to get him,"* Yossarian could never fulfil the criteria for his release from active duty. The more combat missions he flew, the higher his commander raised the threshold.

When *Yossarian* simulated mental illness to escape flying, he was ambushed by the squadron physician, *Doc Daneeka*, who told him that, *"Any pilot requesting mental evaluation for insanity - hoping to be found not sane enough to fly and thereby escape dangerous missions - demonstrates his own sanity in creating the request and thus cannot be declared insane."* Eventually, *Yossarian* realised that he was boxed in when he finally achieved his target and the limit was retroactively raised by his superiors. *So, just when Yossarian figured that he could finally leave the air force base, he discovered that neither his diligence nor feigned madness made an iota of difference.*

It does appear that no matter what we do, we often struggle to break free from malevolent characters who sometimes inhabit the *cuckoo's nest*, which is what life feels like sometimes. Due to our imperfect nature, we have the propensity to engage in certain activities that weaken us. Conversely, there are actions that we ought to undertake that we neglect. This also weakens us. Try to square this conundrum.

And just when I faced the unnerving prospect of spinning my wheels, I discovered that it was time to sign off.

CHAPTER 28

S.T.E.A.M.

On the fly, can you tell the difference between a *nerd* and a *geek*? Until recently, these two words were terms of derision. But, to get on the same page, what do they actually mean?

Although they are virtually synonymous, a sliver of differentiation harks back to their original usage. *Nerd*, or *geek*, refers to someone who may be *"obsessively studious, offbeat, bashful, or socially awkward."* But nowadays, *nerd* confers a degree of pride in single-minded expertise, while *geek* retains its old derogatory reference to eccentric carnival performers. Indeed, the term *computer geek* sums up the contemporary perception of arguably the most high-functioning band of technical performers that exist in the world today.

As *nerds* and *geeks* emerged from laboratories, research departments, and the back-office into daylight, and then entered corporate boardrooms, what type of impact are they having on society and the global economy?

To attempt an answer, it may be useful to recall former schoolmates who were deemed goofy and overly fixated on *S.T.E.M.* (science, technology, engineering and mathematics) subjects. Stereotypically, pupils who were dubbed *swots* or *brainboxes* stood apart and mostly pursued non-mainstream hobbies. In his controversial book titled <u>Unnatural Selection: Why The Geeks Will Inherit The Earth</u>, Mark Roeder explains why people with *geek*-like traits, and high cognitive abilities, overwhelmingly populate the hi-tech industry.

Suddenly, kids who might have been mocked in school and ignored at social functions are now the ones driving the digital revolution. Ostensibly, the poster boy for geeks is none other than B. G., and I'm not referring to one of the *Bee Gees*. Based on the unprecedented pace of technological change, corporate leaders like Jeff Bezos, Elon Musk, Mark Zukerberg, Larry Page and Sergey Brin, would seem to have disproportionate power and influence.

Unfortunately, monitoring mechanisms or, more broadly, adequate regulatory oversight seems to be lacking. Clearly, there is a glaring knowledge gap and mismatch between these tech titans and lawmakers, who we expect to provide ethical and legal guidance for the technology industry. Unwittingly, could we be swapping past hierarchical domination by absolute monarchs, military despots, politicians, and robber barons with the hegemony of tin-eared *nerds?*

To moderate the behaviour and mindset of future generations of technogeeks, there are those who advocate the migration from *S.T.E.M.* to *S.T.E.A.M.* (science, technology, engineering, **arts** and mathematics) - a novel approach to curriculum design. Comparing the two tracks, the American writer Julie Schumacher observed: "*The literature student learns to inquire, to question, to interpret, to critique, to compare, to research, to argue, to sift, to analyse, to shape, to express. His intellect can be put to broad use. The computer major, by contrast, is a technician - a **plumber** clutching a single, albeit shining, box of tools.*"

Essentially, proponents of *S.T.E.A.M.* seek to blunt the rough edges of the so-called *plumbers* with their cutting-edge tools, by steering students away from narrow, technical courses to an integrated curriculum that encompasses the **arts, humanities** and **social sciences**. The aim would be to help youngsters appreciate the complementarity of technical and non-technical disciplines. In the words of another famous *nerd*, Albert Einstein: *"all disciplines and forms of inquiry are 'branches from the same tree.'"* This suggests that knowledge is analogous to multiple branches emanating from a tree trunk which together form the basis of human curiosity.

Left to their devices, many parents would gladly sign off on a vocational-based syllabus centred on, say, computer programming that would provide immediate and guaranteed post-graduation employment for their wards. *"To be, or not to be"*-come a *plumber,* as the *Bard* might have enunciated, or to follow in the footsteps of poet laureate *William Wordsworth,* should however not preclude young minds from inculcating critical thinking, creativity, team work, adaptability, and other soft skills as essential capabilities in a changing world.

No one can predict the future of work with any degree of certainty. Nevertheless, it is indisputable that it will be more digital than analog-driven, implying that tomorrow's in-demand workers will be technically sophisticated. But to avoid a science fiction-inspired *Revenge of the Nerds* scenario, it behoves us to ensure that *S.T.E.M.* adherents acquire the requisite skill sets and emotional intelligence commensurate with the level of responsibilities they are likely to command, going forward. Although he was a controversial figure, no one ever accused the late co-founder of Apple Inc., Steve Jobs, of being a one-dimensional computer *geek*. Over the course of his legendary career, Jobs was able to infuse his company with passion, class and ethereal beauty that permeated Apple's brand and products.

Credited with - or accused of - spinning what was called a *reality distortion field* through the sheer force of his personality, Jobs' opinion of his main rival was very revealing: *"The only problem with Microsoft is they just have no taste, they have absolutely no taste. I don't mean that in a small way. I mean that in a big way, in the sense that they don't think of original ideas and they don't bring much culture into their products."* Tellingly, Jobs' creative flair and famed affinity for calligraphy were emblematic of his status as a *S.T.E.A.M.* maverick who was way ahead of his time.

CHAPTER 29

Elementary

No one knows what goes on in the mind of a designer. Maybe not even the designer does from one moment to the next. That is because we are all furtive organisers who, habitually, feel obliged to order and rearrange our lives, living rooms, right down to our smartphone user interface. Subconsciously, we strive for simplicity and are conditioned to find workarounds within poorly designed habitats. Professionally, there are design practitioners - the most familiar category being industrial product designers - who solve real-life problems and earn a living by creating products and services that compete for our attention. But at a pragmatic level, design is everyone's business.

Studies show that designers are mostly influenced from the outside-inwards or, technically, designers' mental activities respond in a *"world-to-mind direction of fit."* Not only are people interested in what is, but in what could be, by projecting outwards and into the future. As aptly expressed by Richard Buchanan, a US professor and editor of *Design Issues, "Change has always been an essential part of design, because designers are concerned with creating new possibilities in human experience, mediated or facilitated by human-made products."* In general, good designers are those who can operate at the nexus of art and science, possess good observational skills, and follow smart design principles. So, where do design ideas come from?

As humans, our eyes perceive objects in two dimensions, primarily rendered as a circle, triangle, square or rectangle. At normal resolution, we discern straight lines, a corner where two sides meet, flat shapes in two dimensions, and much more. However, through a process called stereophonic imaging, our brains superimpose depth perception which enables us to view objects in three dimensions. Therefore, from our perspective, solid objects are made up of variants of shapes such as a sphere, cylinder, cube, cone and rectangular prism.

From early on in life, intuitively we learn to delineate and de-construct physical structures. Then, using our imagination, we attempt to model elementary patterns from the bottom-up using the same building blocks, as demonstrated by kindergarten children mimicking real life when playing with Lego sets.

Going all the way back to empire builders five thousand years ago, arguably the pinnacle of early antiquity architecture was embodied in Egypt's network of Pyramids. Encompassing a square base and four triangular faces, there are several theories why the Ancient Egyptians chose a pyramid configuration and not, say, a cone or rectangular prism. Amongst Egyptologists, it was widely speculated that *"dead Pharaohs could climb symbolically to the sky and live forever"* or *"the pyramid shape represented the rays of the Sun."*

However, a more mundane explanation could be that, architecturally, the cone shape exceeded their engineering capabilities while a rectangular prism shape would have appeared stodgy and uninspiring. Still, hats off for an awesome engineering feat that involved moving over two million blocks of stone, some weighing as much as ten tons, during the construction of the Great Pyramid of Giza.

More than four thousand years later, the Aztec, Mayan and adjoining civilisations of Central America constructed less grand pyramid monuments with flat tops to harbour and honour their deities. Throughout the ages, an underlying design principle across cultures seems to have revolved around shape and function being inextricably linked. Instinctively, designers seek the synergy between form and function, even if they do not always succeed.

Similar to plane shapes such as triangles and rectangles that are associated with solid structures, curved surfaces are just as easy to conceptualise, but much more difficult to construct in practice. In the past, casting evolved as a true and tested technology, whereby the mould of a complex object is made, followed by a displacement process to produce copies of the original. Across time, the challenge of fabricating non-regular shapes was also taken up by skilled artisans - from carpenters, metalsmiths to stonemasons - who add or subtract from base materials to create a finished product.

In modern times, one of the most striking and groundbreaking architectural designs is the Sydney Opera House (SOH) in Australia. In my mind's eye, SOH's silhouette reminds me of sand dunes, which are crescent-shaped formations with a windward side and a slipface. Sometimes, nothing matches the elegance and majesty of natural phenomena which, with timeless precision, can produce both fragile and highly stable structures that inspire designers.

Conceived by the late Danish architect, Jørn Utzon, in the 1950s, the radical SOH design was a structural masterpiece which was implicitly and geometrically complex. At the time, it could easily have been abandoned without the aid of computer-aided design (CAD) technology. This period coincided with the era of mainframe computers when only governments and well-endowed organisations could access such processing capabilities. Thereafter, the democratisation of digital technology began with the personal computer and culminated in the connectivity enabled by the Internet. Thus, design, like many other areas of human endeavour, migrated from the rudimentary to the industrial and on to the digital age.

Progressively, information technology opened up new opportunities for professional designers, amateurs and hobbyists. CAD and similar tools are primed to boost productivity and creativity, limited only by end-users' imagination. But the ultimate game-changer may be a nascent technology known as additive manufacturing (3D Printing) which empowers users to convert intricate design blueprints into finished products anytime and anywhere in the world, with no holds barred.

CHAPTER 30

Play On

A recent edition of *The Economist* ran an article captioned *The Strange Revival of Vinyl Records.* In all probability, few millennials would have any idea what a vinyl record sounds like. But for an older generation, it is hard to believe that it's been over three decades since cassettes and compact discs (CD) supplanted vinyl, after its century-long domination of the music industry.

Fast-forward to 2004 when the CD peaked at over 90% of volume sales. That year, the rise of MP3 and new streaming services signposted the beginning of the slow decline of digital sound storage media. Although the vinyl footprint was marginal and retail sales had flatlined, yet the medium refused to die. By 2019, *The Economist* estimated that record album sales had risen unexpectedly to 4% of the music market, and surpassed the CD for the first time since 1986. Why the resurgence?

Nostalgia is the obvious, but glib, answer. Certainly, it is a factor but there are more nuanced explanations, such as *demography* and *technology trends*.

For better or worse, in the aftermath of WW2 the cohort of new babies was the largest of its kind in modern history. Defined as those born between 1946 and 1964, the so-called baby-boomer generation *(boomers)* grew up in relative prosperity, if under a frigid nuclear cloud. Discordantly, as the counter-culture movement of the late 1950s and 1960s - exemplified by rock 'n' roll music - tugged at social norms, some aspects of home life remained constant. Back then, the record player was a fixture of the living room static furniture, as were taciturn fathers who rarely lifted a finger around the house. But during the end-of-year holiday season, the dynamics changed.

Suddenly, the old man took charge of stringing up greeting cards and decorating the Christmas tree. In the spirit of goodwill to all, sulky children would clear away their 45 rpm singles and cede territorial control to their father, hoping that his good mood would make him amenable to granting myriad requests. Dusting up his album collection and regaling visitors with songs by the likes of Bing Crosby and Jim Reeves, the glow around the house usually extended into the New Year. Then, the Christmas tree went down and normal routine resumed. That just about summarises a dewy-eyed recollection of the post-WW2 era through a narrow lens.

But wait for it. Unbelievably, in 2006, a horde of front line *boomers* hit the three-score mark. 60! Five years later, many left employment and began to swell the ranks of pensioners. Amazingly, the self-indulgent and mutinous *Beat Generation* had grown up, went mainstream, assumed the mantle of the establishment, and finally became grandparents. The shoe was now on the other foot. Former cultural rebels were now contending with a bewildering post-modernist ideology espoused by their offspring. With the clock ticking down, yet with so much time on their hands, where could they turn? Scour the past for the familiar and trusted, perhaps?

In the event, picture *boomers* with a deserved reputation for moving *demographic needles* rummaging through their closets, salvaging old albums, but discovering that several were irrecoverable. Though enjoying the portability of their digital music players and access to streaming services, some would succumb to an old itch by going out to purchase a turntable. Seeking to recreate that old time feeling when the grandchildren pay a visit, grandpa might underscore protest stories from his youth by holding up his old copy of Bob Dylan's *Highway 61 Revisited.* Pausing to admire the album cover, grandpa may well spin and jitterbug before settling down in his favourite chair.

From barely suppressed smirks to respectful eye-rolls, the grandchildren would politely hang around to share this curious hiss and crackle experience. Bemused by the static noise, the stylus could then get stuck in a worn groove two minutes into the song *"Ballad of A Thin Man."* Startled by a repetition of the same sonic ditty, the poor kids may suddenly realise that grandpa failed to react because he had dozed off!

In his dream world, grandpa perhaps might be re-enacting and recalling his father's snap command: *"Wrench"* from underneath his car bonnet. In those days, many men were car fanatics who sought to bond with their restive sons by waxing lyrical about pistons and carburettors. These fictional anecdotes support the idea that, as well as being psychologically attached to the past, we are also a highly tactile species that loves to tweak and tinker. If, for example, the vision of the driverless vehicle materialises and succeeds in tearing cabbies and truckers away from the steering wheel, what next for those idle hands?

Increasingly, as we transition from an analog to a digital world, it is worth remembering that history is littered with periods when new and more efficient technologies supplanted the old. But, like the fag end of a cigarette left behind after the rest has combusted, traces of old technologies tend to linger. To all intents and purposes, electric and carbon-neutral technologies will soon replace the internal combustion engine which runs on fossil fuels. Similarly, digital watches, electronic books and digital cameras have made significant inroads into the watch-making, publishing and photographic industries, respectively. One thing is clear - technological progress is rarely, if ever, reversed.

Yet, long after an old technology has passed its sell-by date and become sufficiently quaint to deserve a hallowed spot in a museum, usually there are holdouts who strive to keep the legacy alive. For example, after motor vehicles displaced horse-drawn carriages, horses bolstered pastimes like show jumping, thoroughbred racing and polo, all preserves of the well-heeled.

Turning full circle, the recent spurt in vinyl sales highlighted by *The Economist* was not a unique phenomenon, but part of a trend. In popular culture, people who venerate items like mechanical wristwatches, leather-bound books, original paintings, vintage vehicles, and retro turntables, are caricatured as *long in the tooth* conservatives. No kidding!

CHAPTER 31

Hubris

In *No Country for Old Men,* retired Lt. Col. Carson Wells was hired to hunt down a homicidal maniac, Anton Chigurh. Incidentally, both men were Vietnam War veterans, and Wells knew how utterly depraved Chigurh was. Nevertheless, he took the job because he needed the money, and misguidedly believed that he was smarter than Chigurh. He was not.

Sure enough, the hunted outmanoeuvred the hunter. In their final scene together, Chigurh held a full-bore shotgun while sitting across from his hot and cornered prey. In his cryptic rhetoric that dripped with contempt, Chigurh asked Wells, *"All right. Let me ask you something. If the rule you followed brought you to this, of what use was the rule?"* Wells retorted, *"Do you have any idea how crazy you are?"* Crazy Chigurh might have been, but Wells' so-called *rule* presupposed that he always overstepped to see how far he could push the envelope. Right until the moment his luck ran out, Wells had lived a charmed life but, in the end, his trademark swagger could not save him from his nemesis.

Switching gears, before he could be removed from office by the US Congress, Richard Nixon in 1974 became the first and only incumbent to resign as US President. In a revealing interview three years later with the British journalist David Frost, Nixon's mask slipped when he made this stunning remark, *"Well, when the president does it, that means it is not illegal."* Regardless of context, this was quite an extraordinary statement by a lawyer-turned-politician who was accused of abuse of power, obstruction of justice, and contempt of Congress.

In a political career spanning decades, Nixon was nicknamed *"Tricky Dick"* during an earlier senate race, and might have operated under the illusion that he was above the law and could therefore breach conventional rules. Too late, Nixon discovered that, in a constitutional republic based on the separation of powers, no elected officeholder possessed unlimited power.

There is a direct line connecting these narratives to the ancient Greek mythology of Icarus and his father, Daedalus. As a renowned craftsman, Daedalus had designed wings from feathers and wax that would help his son escape to Crete. Before take-off, his father had warned Icarus not to fly too low to avoid the sea's dampness, or too high. Perhaps Icarus should have listened to his father and split the difference; rather, he ignored Daedalus' counsel and flew too close to the Sun. Tragically, the wax melted, Icarus plunged into the sea and drowned. Like Carson Wells, Icarus could not resist the adrenaline rush of testing the boundaries, to his eternal regret.

Of course, time never stands still. Who knows how many people have since failed to learn from Icarus' fate. But, truly, hubris can be an intoxicating drug that some find difficult to resist, no less so in this age of rapid transformation.

In January 2000, America Online (AOL) was a popular web portal at the forefront of the 1990s' Internet boom with about 25 million online subscribers. Riding the wave of dot-com optimism, AOL's market capitalisation rose to $164 billion, which was an insane valuation for a 15-year old company with few tangible assets. By contrast, Time Warner was a media conglomerate with cable and publishing assets, including huge libraries of movie and television content. Incongruously, Time Warner's market value was about 60% of AOL's. A proposed merger of the two companies would gain Time Warner access to AOL's subscriber base. Subsequently, the bubble burst, even as AOL's dial-up service was losing out to faster broadband networks.

By the time the dust settled, the merged company declared an eye-popping $99 billion loss in 2002, while AOL's relative value nosedived by 87% from its peak. Just as badly mauled was Time Warner and, at the time, the AOL Time Warner combination was adjudged as the most awful in corporate history. Possibly the most high-profile victim of this saga was Ted Turner, the founder of CNN, who had sold his company to Time Warner and became the largest individual shareholder of AOL Time Warner. Perhaps Turner and his board of directors overreached. They should have heeded their old-school instincts rather than succumb to the market frenzy that wiped out trillions of dollars in stock market wealth.

Today, there is a growing belief that social media is a double-edged bet. Naively, at first people welcomed the promise of universal connectivity, and it was free to boot. Despite the early surge in innovation, the most dominant player, Facebook, soon gobbled up its nearest rivals. With about 2.4 billion users, or 37.5% of the world's population outside China, a scary pattern emerged. Without much thought or reflection, people broke a *rule*, a private rule that defied common sense. Ignoring all possible consequences, subscribers compromised their privacy and allowed Facebook to harvest intimate personal data at the core of their being. Now, social media platforms have made facts and false information indistinguishable, thereby weaponising and propagating digital poison.

Recapping, Carson Wells and Icarus met untimely ends, which must have been a shock to their associates. In Richard Nixon's resignation speech, he couched his fall from grace thus, *"... only if you have been in the deepest valley can you ever know how magnificent it is to be on the highest mountain."* &%*!? Sometime in 2009, Time Warner finally spun off AOL, and returned to its roots. With respect to Facebook and other social media companies, their anomalous impact on our future is still up in the air.

Overshadowing these calamities is a full-bore threat hanging over us like the sword of Damocles. Since the invention of the atomic bomb in the 1940s, efforts were undertaken to curb nuclear proliferation but the paranoia, and hubris, of nuclear states is palpable. Sadly, the likelihood of a nuclear weapons-free world is as remote as ever. In which case, to paraphrase Chigurh, *"Let me ask you a direct question. If the logic we followed set us on the road to nuclear Armageddon, of what ultimate value is human logic?"*

CHAPTER 32

Crestfallen

Lauded as the *King of Beasts* and *King of Birds,* respectively, lions and eagles are fearsome alpha predators atop the food chain. Both are living proof of the savagery and, paradoxically, the intrinsic beauty in creation. Watching a maned lion strut across the savannah at dusk or an eagle soar effortlessly out of sight can take the breath away. So regal, awe-inspiring, and oblivious of external validation are they, that humans have extolled them for ages.

From ancient Mesopotamia to the Middle Ages, and beyond, the lion has long been associated with sovereigns and the aristocracy, who shamelessly appropriated the lion's stardust. Consider the intriguing case of King Henry I who, in 1100 AD, added the lion to the royal banner of England, then co-opted a second from his wife's family. By 1154 AD, two lions became three, courtesy of King Henry II.

Empires like Persia and Rome, on their part, celebrated the eagle as a symbol of courage and divinity. The German coat of arms features a muscle-flexing black eagle with a red beak and red feet. Not to be outdone, Russia incorporated the double-headed eagle in its official emblem. Last but not the least, the seal of the United States projects the bald eagle as a mark of "freedom, *liberty, strength, power and* majesty."

Although lions are indigenous to the tropics and numerous species of eagles dot continents, the traditions of diverse cultures allude to the creatures' nobility, mystique and legend. Lions may appear languid but few natural phenomena can match the sudden explosion of a crouched lion's onslaught. Yet, lions are known to spend 80% of each day asleep, patrol at night to protect prides, prefer to hunt solo, but leave heavy chores like food sourcing and taking care of the young to lionesses. If any of this sounds familiar, reflect on the lifestyle of the privileged ruling class. But to prove their superiority as the ultimate predators, royals often made a big show of hunting and bagging lions as trophies, wisely from a safe distance.

Notably, the eagle is renowned for being able to glide to heights that other birds cannot reach, which enables it to build its nest at discrete locations. From its vaunted perch, and with eyesight that is up to five times better than human vision, the eagle can spot its prey from afar, swoop in at incredible speed, and attack with its talons. When breeding, a female eagle usually lays two eggs. After hatching, a grotesque process unfolds whereby the stronger of the newborns often kills its kin without the parents batting an eyelid.

In short, lions and eagles are highly efficient killing machines that are universally admired for their power, audacity, ruthlessness, independence, and imperious aura. On a planet noted for its *survival of the fittest* doctrine, early humans may have drawn pragmatic lessons from nature to ensure their survival. However, as human beings evolved and became more civilised, should we really continue to live according to the dogma of aggression and barbarity?

The pacifist gesture of stripping the images of lions and eagles from institutions' coats of arms, crests and banners is obviously very radical, and possibly naive. No doubt, the idea would leave many traditionalists crestfallen and may rattle the cages of power hogs. Mind you, how many hereditary rulers and old-fashioned monarchs with real power are left anywhere? But, given that the world remains highly militarised and operates under the principle of *might is right*, will anything ever change? Not only are military strategists always fighting the *last war*, for long the mindset hardly shifted from bygone days when armies deployed soldiers wielding swords and shields, and fought toe-to-toe, nose-to-nose on blood-soaked battlefields. Those were the days when it paid to look and fight like a *lionheart*. A century ago, when military aviation commenced, many pilots proudly depicted the eagle on their aircraft fuselage. Now what?

Increasingly, the world's most powerful nations are building and deploying lethal pilot-less drones. They are also designing and testing autonomous fighting troops, essentially robots, which are programmed to destroy enemy combatants. It is therefore possible to envision a future when armed forces will activate elite commando units on special missions, while infantry soldiers and pilots would operate joysticks attached to digital workstations. Of course, old-fashioned shooting wars will continue in poorer regions of the world, whereas the big powers dare not confront each other for fear of triggering a nuclear exchange.

In my opinion, the world has two choices: to pursue global peace or to live under the constant threat of mass and indiscriminate destruction. On the face of it, the former sounds utopian and unrealistic, since it would take the wisdom of Solomon to negotiate total and verifiable nuclear disarmament. On the other hand, the calculus of the *next world war* does not compute, simply because it *cannot be fought and won*. Remember that the humiliated 'losing' side will still possess residual warheads and motivation to destroy the world many times over. So, what alternative do we have? I have a token, anti-war, proposal.

On the implausible path to global harmony, let us replace the lion with a lamb and the eagle with a dove, their temperamental opposites. By symbolically breaking from the past, at least future generations will have a more positive frame of reference. Maybe, someday, we will finally realise that the meek are indeed destined to inherit the earth.

>>>>><<<<<

CHAPTER 33

Antsy

Work-life balance has been a controversial water-cooler topic of discussion since the 1980s. Prior to that decade, the impact of *work-family conflict* had been studied for over a hundred years. What caused the change in semantics and, more broadly, how have we adapted to the dichotomy between toil and leisure?

Pre-industrial age, there was hardly any barrier between work and family because most people lived off the land, and it was effectively all hands on deck. Highly labour-intensive, subsistence farming and animal husbandry demanded all-day, year-round attention and, in addition to family members, extra hands often pitched in at harvest time. Mining was an occupation that was almost exclusively male-dominated, and required men to spend time away from home in very brutal working conditions. But, at least, their womenfolk knew precisely where they were and would usually welcome them home to a hot bath and a ready meal.

Industrialisation set in motion the so-called *work-family conflict* since it drew manual workers into factories where 14 to 16-hour workdays were not unusual. Even their supervisors and line managers were expected to work overtime at peak periods. In those days, the division of responsibilities between husbands and wives was sharply defined. Still, the long hours spent by spouses in formal employment created tension in family relationships.

In time, trade unions fought for improved workers' rights until the standard 40-hour work-week was enshrined into law. Despite this, the wrangle on the home front did not abate. It turned out that men revelled in a rugged work culture and were drawn to red-blooded pastimes such as clubbing and gambling. Also, the stereotypical man reckoned that his promotion prospects improved by logging long hours or participating in after-hours drinking.

Post-WW2, educational opportunities and birth-control empowerment untethered women from the home. By the 1970s, dual-income families became commonplace and many women embraced the tenets of the feminist movement. As more women entered the workplace, the *work-family conflict* outcry mutated into an agitation for *work-life balance*. Male-centric work environments were not necessarily designed to accommodate new mothers or women with young children. In other words, female employees faced an institutionalised *imbalance* between family and career pursuits, the characteristics of which were largely different from those experienced by men.

Perhaps fortuitously, the advocacy for *work-life balance* overlapped with the *post-industrial age*. The age of acceleration introduced the personal computer, global connectivity, and other digital technologies that have enabled flexitime and telecommuting. The unintended consequence of continuous accessibility has however resulted in workers becoming more stressed to such an extent that, rather than the pendulum being in balance, many feel trapped on a kinetic see-saw.

Not long ago, I came across an article titled *"Ants Understand Work-Life Balance."* Ants? Really?

People who live in warm climates encounter ants in their kitchens and around the house, whereas in more temperate climes, insects spend the cooler seasons hibernating out of sight. By and large, tens of thousands of different ant species live in highly-organised ant colonies and most of them are probably oblivious of human activities. When we speculate about advanced alien civilisations, we gaze out into outer space, while ignoring other life forms with which we share our planet. Ants, for instance, possess acute and very robust communication faculties that we do not fully understand. Hence, when we swoon over our smartphones, is it possible that there are organisms that are able to communicate naturally by telepathy?

So, what can we learn from ants about *work-life balance?* For starters, it helps to know that ants are classified as *workers*, *soldiers*, fertile males called *drones*, and a handful of fertile females known as *queens*. Studies have shown that ants live in social organisations that manifest advanced defence and resource utilisation attributes. Like humans, ants foster production through division of labour and, collectively, are able to solve intricate problems.

Researchers at Missouri University of Science and Technology in the US discovered that ants have a propensity to optimise energy and resource allocation within each colony. Typically, while designated ants are hard at work, another group remains inactive, thereby conserving food and capacity. As the population grows, a larger proportion stays dormant based on the principle that productive ants spend five times as much energy as those at rest. On occasions when demand rises for defence or maintenance duties, inactive ants are called into service.

Ostensibly, conscientious ants possess better conservation instincts than humans who seem to always want to eat their cake and have it. Unlike ants, humans do not shut down brain and body functions when *chillaxing* (chilling out and relaxing). Instead, when we start feeling antsy at work, we yearn for leisure activities - from sports and recreation to dynamic holidaying - which tend to increase the pressure on global resources and the environment. Conversely, ants appear to be motivated less by *work-life balance* than achieving *energy balance* within their ecosystem.

Translated into our domain, we could begin by paying judicious attention to how we expend energy at work, at leisure, and in between. And with laser focus on productivity improvement and change management, technology could very well serve as a vehicle for seamless *work-life integration*.

CHAPTER 34

Gumption

From cradle to grave, in season and out of season, we solve problems. That is our lot. Life throws many at us but often we do a fairly good job of digging ourselves into holes.

At birth, babies bring both joy and mild chaos into their parents' lives. Toddlers are little broncos that must be tamed for their own sake. Adolescents and teenagers can develop into well-adjusted souls or choose to become human flame-throwers. Under the veneer of maturity, adults excel at creating disorder despite their best intentions. Habitually, young people blame their parents for all the world's problems but, unerringly, the cycle repeats itself generation after generation. All told, human stewardship has neither produced a utopia or a state of total dystopia. Each age, each year, each minute throws up its own web of interlocking curveballs that leave us wheezing and sometimes breathless.

Contemporary human development indices show that the arc of economic progress has widened, but at what cost? On the big issues such as social injustice, religious conflicts, water and food security, immigration and demographic trends, and climate change, has it been a case of two steps forward, and one step back? To be fair, when problems loom large and appear intractable, people feel helpless and instinctively shift the responsibility to governments and multilateral institutions like the United Nations.

When faced with personal complications and life's infinite imponderables, it is much harder to pass the buck. Left to our devices, it is very easy to coast through life by plying the path of least resistance. And unless pushed to the wall, most of us toss and turn within our comfort zone, and are prone to procrastination in stressful situations. However, a purposeful life entails occasionally setting stretch goals that test the limits of our capabilities. At our best, we are capable of amazing exploits, as reflected in our ability to solve very complex problems. It is therefore not surprising that we would develop a generic framework for creative problem-solving, defined as *"the cognitive process of seeking an original or novel solution to a problem."*

Quite wrongly, the creative terrain is often assumed to be the exclusive preserve of gifted individuals. However, the great American inventor, Thomas Edison, asserted that *"genius is one percent inspiration and ninety-nine percent perspiration."* In other words, nothing exceptional comes easy but rather requires sustained effort to accomplish. All of us have it in us to pursue lofty goals, and to exceed all expectations, if we learn to solve problems imaginatively.

In a hypothetical scenario in which a random selection of people recounted the toughest challenge they ever faced, expectedly their responses will mirror their personal circumstances. However, imagine if we designed an experiment whereby the same group, on a journey of self-discovery and character-building, was asked to: *"Locate the heaviest burden within reach and carry it."*

To help them along, let us equate the *"heaviest burden"* to the maximum weight each participant can lift relative to their body weight. The objective is not to turn them into professional weightlifters but, by a sleight of hand, to illustrate a structured and creative approach to problem-solving.

First, be clear what the problem is and rephrase it, if necessary, for optimum clarity. Next, research and analyse the problem, then evaluate alternative solutions. Having done so, the most common error is to select an immediate solution. In this case, proceed by learning the basics of weightlifting such as maintaining the right posture to avoid the risk of injury. When bending the knees or squatting, the back must be kept straight, while the head and spine also must be in a straight line. It is important to train relevant muscle groups in a slow and methodical manner so as to stimulate the muscles for growth and adaptation. It cannot be overemphasised that a warm-up exercise at the beginning of a routine helps to prevent injury caused by cold muscles.

At the outset, it is wise not to rush but to attempt a light load before progressing to increasingly heavier weights. Novices tend to hold their breath continuously, rather than breathing out when lifting, and breathing in when lowering the weights. In any creative process, the *feedback loop* may be the most salient device available to us. This involves a series of conscious and non-conscious mental activities that oscillate between an individual's thought process and the sensory signals being received. Within the context of a weightlifting process, pay attention to any sign of acute pain transmitted by the central nervous system. Also, having a role model can serve as a form of inspiration during rough patches.

Over time, tracking incremental progress ensures that *"what gets measured gets improved,"* until the objective is fulfilled. In summary, teaching points include: | *be well-informed | avoid procrastination but do not rush | develop resilience | be intuitive and have a positive attitude | leverage feedback | whatever you do, stay safe (don't break your back!)*.

Stopping short of calling him a role model, a surprisingly creative problem-solver was the enigmatic but highly resourceful Forrest Gump. Weighed down by life, Gump had the decks stacked against him at birth, and was not expected to amount to much. A wry twist on Gump's favourite put-down of his detractors was *"smart is as smart does,"* implying that we should be judged based on our actions and not by appearance. Blessed with an indomitable fighting spirit, he prevailed in life partly due to his calm but tenacious disposition.

In many ways, Gump made his own luck - hightailing it when danger lurked, upending the shrimp industry, demonstrating *Bubba*-sized integrity, investing in a "fruit" company *(Apple)* to taking a punt on love and fatherhood. Whenever he received negative feedback, he recalibrated and had the gumption to get right back up. Forrest Gump may have appeared ham-fisted, but he was not a quitter and would always carry the heaviest load he could find with equanimity.

CHAPTER 35

Startup On A Pittance

A generation or two ago, the bedrock of what constituted entrepreneurship was a far cry from our 21st century perspective. An older perspective, which emanated from the *Industrial Revolution* and persisted for much of the last century, was centred on the so-called 3Ms; that is, *man*, *machine* and *money*. After the computer age commenced in the 1950s, *information* gained greater currency and would later become as indispensable as the 3Ms. In fact, some would argue that information technology is now more potent than *machine*, and just as important as *money*.

If the return on capital invested is a yardstick for the success of a business venture, it would take an exceptional entrepreneur to build a promising business on a pittance, defined here as seed money not exceeding $100. It is not impossible but, most definitely, it would demand extraordinary business acumen, discipline and perseverance. Although $100 might suffice for a creative hobby, this amount represents a mere pittance in a bid to build a truly viable business.

Computer Revolution

By happy coincidence, the democratisation of computer technology in the wake of the personal computer revolution, starting in the 1980s, changed the world irrevocably. Comprising basic hardware and software components, the process of computer programming or coding in particular empowered a whole generation of young people, who went on to take the world by storm. Names such as Bill Gates, Steve Wozniak, Larry Page, Sergey Brin, to mention a few, and the companies they co-founded - Microsoft, Apple and Google, respectively - redefined entrepreneurship and signalled a paradigm shift in the wealth creation process. More recently, social media platforms such as Facebook, Instagram, Snapchat, Twitter, and many others have similarly transformed how we interact and work.

Digital Age

Given that we now live in the digital age, perhaps it is reasonable to assume that most people possess a smartphone, and a high proportion have access to laptop or desktop computers. Without these basic tools, it is difficult to imagine how anyone can participate meaningfully in the modern, fast-paced economy. What is remarkable about these gadgets is that they serve as essential communication tools, as well as channels for money-making for those with the skills and creativity to harness their power.

From the foregoing, it is now possible to start a business online, especially since superfast broadband is now affordable and widely available in homes, offices and public places. Outside of professional coders and software engineers, opportunities to exploit *information* as a building block of entrepreneurship abound. So, with a computer, broadband connection and $100 or less in your pocket, let us explore some business opportunities that are particularly germane.

Podcasting

Blogging has been around for much longer, but surveys show that an increasing number of people enjoy listening to podcasts rather than text-based, long form blogs. The obvious advantage of the latter is that end-users generally can consume podcasts while engaged in other activities; in other words, they are able multitask. Another surprising finding was that consumers conveniently and routinely listen to hours of audio content, contrary to what might be expected from people who would normally exhibit a short attention span.

For about $50, it is possible to acquire a microphone of decent quality, including a pop filter for less than $20 needed to suppress extraneous sounds. Connection to the USB port of a laptop enables easy plug-and-play and recording capabilities. *Audacity* is a popular, open-source software application that can be downloaded free of charge, and serves as an audio editing tool.

Starting a podcast from scratch provides an avenue for building a brand, and the potential to reach a wide audience using an audio format. Often, podcasters identify their market niche, and then tailor their content to meet the demand. An approach to monetizing a podcast involves partnering with companies seeking to promote their products and services. Typically, the podcaster would run messages from sponsors at the beginning and end of each podcast episode.

Vlogging

YouTube grew so fast in less than two decades such that the world's most popular video-sharing platform displaced traditional television in many people's viewing habits. The fact that *YouTube* accommodates and promotes user-generated content has also been a stroke of genius.

Becoming a vlogger requires little more than access to a decent video camera which a good smartphone or tablet provides. A vlog is a quintessential multimedia medium that combines video, text and audio content to produce motion picture. As long as end-users do not contravene the platform's rules, they can upload and distribute self-generated content without much hindrance. Similar to podcasters, vloggers operate channels on *YouTube* that enable content playback on a diverse range of devices, from desktop computers, laptops, tablets to smartphones.

Vlogging attracts both amateur and professional video producers, several of whom have succeeded in starting successful careers. Depending on partner program criteria, *YouTube* uses sophisticated algorithms that convert viewing statistics into monetary value. Anecdotal evidence indicates that top-earning vloggers, including many early adopters, pull in six to seven-figure dollar incomes per annum.

Online Tutoring

Instead of free-form vlogging, tutoring is a structured and well-formatted approach to online learning. This business rests largely on the expertise, in specific domains, of the tutor to disseminate knowledge to a broad audience.

Using a slide and audio presentation format, including visual cues, the demand for online tutoring has risen steadily over the years. Not surprisingly, many subjects that at first glance appear somewhat esoteric, find a ready audience on the Internet. This suggests that intellect rather than money may be the most crucial input required by contemporary tutors wishing to start a business. Disciplined entrepreneurs with specialized skills can convert their knowledge into downloadable content that can be monetized for the benefit of diverse cohorts of learners.

Online Seller

For those with a knack for e-commerce, the auction website, eBay, offers a robust and trusted platform for trading a wide range of products.

eBay built a well-regulated environment that has attracted legions of merchants that have, in turn, built successful businesses of varying sizes. However, the auction market also lends itself to the aspiration of many participants who view it as an opportunity to make money on the side. In essence, some sellers start out small, and operate at the margins while others, bitten by the eBay bug, hunker down and grow into sizeable businesses.

Airbnb Host

Airbnb is a poster child for the sharing economy which has grown into a global brand in short order. Based on a straightforward premise of optimizing liveable space, becoming a business partner depends on complying with the company's guidelines.

Unless one owns an array of properties, many Airbnb hosts fall into the category of passive single-resident partners who seek to make extra money on a periodic or seasonal basis.

In conclusion…

In terms of traditional ventures that may not require significant monetary outlay, examples abound. The delivery business is a major component of the gig economy, and anyone with an idle vehicle can easily leverage this asset. Becoming a direct sales representative of a company is another up-voted suggestion on the Internet.

The laundry and ironing service may not be glamorous yet, if you are able-bodied, this is one old-fashioned occupation that either provides short-term relief or could be expanded into a respectable business.

Testers and reviewers represent a new breed of *work from home* individuals who assist traditional manufacturers and digitally-driven businesses to test their products. Anyone who is conscientious and highly disciplined can explore opportunities in this space.

In conclusion, lack of seed capital has ceased to be a barrier to starting a new business. There are scores of entrepreneurial ideas that have proven their mettle at a moment in history when intangible software is as valuable, if not more so, than tangible hardware. While not everyone can aspire to become a computer programmer, nevertheless information technology has opened up innumerable and new frontiers for budding entrepreneurs that did not exist a generation ago.

CHAPTER 36

Timeout On Dirty Energy

The Beijing National Stadium, otherwise known as the *Bird's Nest*, is an architectural masterpiece that hosted the 2008 Summer Olympics. Despite the arena's magnificence, Beijing 2008 was rated as the most polluted Games in history. The level of toxic smog encountered by spectators was three times higher than at the Atlanta Olympics held twelve years earlier.

To their credit, Chinese authorities restricted vehicular movement, shuttered factories and constrained construction projects prior to the quadrennial sporting event, in a forlorn attempt to lower pollution levels. But reputations die hard. Members of the US Cycling Team caused a diplomatic faux pas by showing up at Beijing

Capital International Airport wearing face masks, in what remained one of the most indelible images beamed from China that summer.

Wuhan, China

Almost twelve years later, China would once again attract global attention. This time around, face masks remained firmly in the line of sight, but under radically different circumstances.

Late 2019, news slowly seeped out of China about a human-to-human transmissible novel coronavirus that was traced to Wuhan, the capital of Hubei Province. In response, the city of 11 million people was completely locked down by China's central government. Television screens showed swarms of ordinary citizens in face masks and healthcare workers wearing personal protective equipment. Suddenly, a Chinese city was not under siege from soot particles, but a more pernicious killer in the form of Covid-19.

Global Lockdown

By the close of the first quarter of 2020, the coronavirus crisis had spread to over 180 countries across the globe. Initially wrong-footed by its speed of transmission, nations soon rallied and reacted by imposing travel bans, restricting economic activity, and foisting social-distancing and lockdown directives on their hapless citizens.

Having experienced *SARS* and *MERS* epidemics within the last two decades, Asian countries were quicker off the blocks. Meanwhile, Italy and Spain bore the initial brunt in Europe, but since then no continent except Antarctica has been exempted. Culturally, the wearing of face masks had become commonplace in the Far East, but less so in other parts of the world. Assailed by powerful critics, the World Health Organization (WHO) struggled valiantly to coordinate a global response. Officially, the body issued periodic guidelines to alleviate the devastating impact of the pandemic on everyday life.

Before long, the majority of the world's population was in lockdown, an unprecedented event that disrupted the global supply chain and upended economic activities.

Pollution Lull

Under these unsettling conditions, the bulk of the world's fleet of commercial aircraft was grounded, forcing the travel and tourism industry to its knees.

Although power plants continued to electrify cities and homes, non-essential businesses were shut down, in compliance with governments' physical distancing policy.

With Covid-19 casting a pall of doom and gloom, a surprising silver lining was the dramatic reduction - as much as 60% - in air pollution levels in some of the worst affected countries. Evidently, a disproportionate number of such cities are located in China and South Asia, including India, Pakistan and Bangladesh. Despite being signatories to the Paris Climate Agreement (PCA), India and China are notorious for their penchant for coal-fired power plants, which they continue to build and roll out.

Rather incongruously amidst a virulent pandemic, newspaper pictures spotlighted the famous *Taj Mahal*, located in the city of Agra, India, regal and gleaming in sunlight for the first time in living memory. Prior to this crisis, the original white marble had long acquired a yellow and green hue, due to its proximity to an unremitting swirl of car fumes and industrial pollutants.

Relatively clean air patterns, similar to Agra's, were experienced in several countries, and photographs were published to highlight the transformation. However, despite this welcome respite in places like New Delhi, Karachi, Jinan and Xinxiang, industrial activity might simply revert to the norm once the lockdown was lifted.

By the same token, the physical constraints imposed globally meant that a high percentage of the world's estimated 1.4 billion motor vehicles clammed up for weeks on end. As a result, pollution maps showed dramatic improvements in air quality. Equally, a Europe-wide study during the first month of the stay-at-home order reported 11,000 fewer deaths that were attributed to cleaner air. There was also a reduction in the number of new asthma sufferers. Based on statistical models, the authors of the study stressed the benefits that could accrue globally if the reliance on fossil fuels was curtailed.

Of course, the world did not need the pandemic confinement to establish the link between the burning of fossil fuels and air quality. Consequently, it may be worthwhile to assess the impact of the global economic slowdown on the hydrocarbon industry, which is largely responsible for greenhouse gas emissions and adverse climate change.

Market Glut

Unsurprisingly, the decrease in global demand for fossil fuels, especially crude oil, reached its nadir during the Covid-19 crisis. In the recent past, US shale oil producers had become a counterweight to the international oil cartel, the Organization of Petroleum Exporting Countries (OPEC). With the global oil markets in a flux, sharp disagreements between OPEC members, and with other oil-producing nations, particularly Russia, had signalled a slowing market.

When the crisis hit, demand for oil declined sharply thus precipitating a steep drop in prices. Attempts by the leading players to stave off a complete collapse were too little, too late. Having lost control, the price per barrel of the benchmark West Texas Intermediate futures fell below $0 for the first time in history. Incredibly, major marketers were running out of storage space, implying that producers were being forced to shut down oil wells.

For oil-producing nations, the situation had turned into a nightmare. For retail consumers, this turn of events was a cause for celebration, if temporary, as pump prices plunged. And for climate change activists, this represented an opportunity to keep hydrocarbons like crude oil, gas and coal in the ground to limit ongoing damage to the environment. From the perspective of the proponents of renewable energy, the picture was more nuanced.

Renewable Energy

Carbon emission levels had recently soared, as China powered its way into becoming the world's second largest economy. India and other emerging economies were not far behind, thus increasing global energy demand, primarily in manufacturing, transportation, and electric power generation. In turn, climate scientists began to sound alarm bells about global warming, and worsening climate conditions, caused by unsustainable levels of carbon dioxide and methane emissions.

To mitigate these negative trends, a clamour for alternative energy sources grew. However, renewable energy from sunlight, wind, geothermal heat, ocean waves, and the like, remained uncompetitive relative to fossil fuels. Nevertheless, over the last decade, technology and price breakthroughs, combined with government subsidies, heralded the push for the so-called *Green Deal*. In short, the ambition underpinning this proposal was for economies to gradually decarbonize their economies and seek to become carbon-neutral in the coming decades. To achieve this goal, nations were encouraged to migrate towards electric vehicles, solar and wind power generation, innovative battery technologies, low-carbon manufacturing, and potentially, carbon tariff regimes. Alas, following major mishaps at Chernobyl and Fukushima, the nuclear energy sector has remained on the back burner for wary policymakers.

The overarching impetus for the global community to embrace the *Green Deal* and similar initiatives was encapsulated in the 2016 PCA which sought to limit the average increase in global temperature to 1.5°C. Failure to do so was couched in dire existential predictions for our planet, hence the sense of urgency. Unfortunately, the incumbent US president, at the helm of the world's largest economy and second biggest polluter, is a climate change sceptic who engineered his country's exit from the PCA. Against all logic, the US president has continued to champion dirty energy sources, especially coal, as a sop to his political base.

Despite these setbacks, all the signs point to a future that cannot be held back indefinitely. Following the collapse in crude oil prices, potentially this could hurt renewable energy initiatives, by making the sector less competitive in the near term. Furthermore, the priorities of many nations might change in the aftermath of Covid-19, characterized by huge stimulus packages and rising debts, which could engender a reduction in domestic subsidies for renewables. On the other hand, this crisis could be a turning point for investors who are being offered a golden opportunity to invest in energy sources of the future. Under this scenario, the handwriting may be on the wall for OPEC as an entity. Not only will its clout diminish, but countries like Venezuela and Nigeria will soon have their backs to the wall, unless they manage to diversify their economies away from oil exports.

Certainly, fossil fuels will remain in the mix for a while, but smart money should be betting on new technologies, jobs of the future, and a more sustainable economic order. As many analysts have noted, this pandemic could turn out to be as momentous as the two world wars, after which sweeping changes occurred. To save our planet and ensure that the global economy is repurposed and repositioned for the new millennium, now may be the ideal time to finally supplant dirty energy with cleaner energy. Until this transition becomes irreversible, the world should take a deep breath, and embrace change for the sake of generations to come.

CHAPTER 37

Erosion of Middle-Class Jobs

An incessant cry emitted in several countries these past decades lamented the hollowing out of well-paying middle-class jobs. On top of that, many working class and blue-collar employees experienced wage stagnation. Although workers generally upskilled, as information technology and process innovation engendered productivity gains, research studies suggested that virtually all the financial benefits during this period accrued to investors and the owners of capital.

Lucky for some, but whatever did happen to those solid middle-class jobs?

Job Classifications

It has long been construed that the backbone of a thriving democratic society is its middle-class workforce. Any government that trifles with the interests of this cadre of workers could therefore be asking for trouble. Trouble usually comes in various guises, but the most decisive is often at the ballot box.

Aside from matters hinging on war and peace, democratic elections are usually decided on issues centred on the pocketbook. In mature democracies, the middle-class headcount makes up the bulk of the electorate, where elections are typically won and lost. Growing the middle class and keeping it happy is therefore a prudent governing strategy. But even autocratic regimes learn to be wary when handling hot-button issues concerning the middle class.

Although the definition of what constitutes middle class may vary from country to country based on income levels, however there are some fundamental similarities in the characteristics of middle-class jobs.

First and foremost, white-collar professionals like lawyers, physicians, engineers, management consultants, accountants and bankers are sometimes bracketed as upper middle class. But, in reality, the majority of them belong in the middle class. In addition, marketers, salesmen, educators, civil servants, brokers, administrators, nurses, and small business owners are also classified as members of this upwardly-mobile group.

In the real sector, one of the greatest post-World War II economic achievements was the elevation of blue-collar personnel in manufacturing industries into stable, well-paying, middle-class status. This conferred economic power and social prestige on such employees. In this category are, for example, car and construction workers, and long-haul truck drivers.

By the way, an oft-overlooked fact of history is that manufacturing jobs were once at the bottom of the pecking order. It took a while for employers to agree wage increases for blue-collar workers but, by putting more money in the pockets of their workforce, the resulting impact on the overall economy was immense and sustained.

Globalisation

Numerous business trends were already set in motion before the end of the *Cold War* in 1989. However, the coming in from the cold of former Communist states, and the earlier opening up of China, accelerated these trends and galvanized the ascendancy of free market reforms globally. Even India, which had endured stultifying socialist policies since independence, introduced crucial liberal reforms in 1991. With a combined population representing about a third of the world's total, China would go on to become the *workshop of the world* while India's hordes of engineers were able to showcase their skill sets in a global market.

Outsourcing and Offshoring

Post-1989, the free movement of people, as well as massive capital flows enabled by technology, caught the attention of investors everywhere. Aided by the business mantra of realizing the highest shareholder value possible, company executives revised their business models to take advantage of low-wage labour in remote corners of the world.

Before long, China became a vibrant manufacturing hub for countless products - everything from machinery, home appliances, to toys. As good-quality but inexpensive Chinese products flooded branded retail stores in the US and elsewhere, the competitive landscape was being radically transformed.

Offshoring of manufacturing jobs from the heartland of developed economies to the Far East became commonplace, with the resulting expansion and integration of supply chains. For instance, except for bespoke production, the textile industry shifted almost entirely to Asia. Apart from countries like Bangladesh and Vietnam that were able to compete with China labour-wise, this most traditional of industries became a shadow of itself in much of the rest of the world.

In the case of India, its low-wage but technically proficient engineers attracted the attention of large corporations that set up or relocated their call centres and data entry operations away from their home base. From this modest beginning, India's critical mass of highly skilled software engineers would go on to establish technology firms like Infosys and

Wipro that now rival their Western counterparts, in terms of technical sophistication and brand identity.

Trending Down

There is no escaping the fact that offshoring and outsourcing practices have had a devastating effect on large swathes of middle-class jobs in the West. To be sure, the availability of cheap imports benefited consumers everywhere and crucially helped to dampen inflationary pressures, but the net effect has been the wholesale disruption of millions of manufacturing jobs.

In the ensuing rubble, it became fashionable to refer in a derogatory manner to the replacement of manufacturing jobs with catch-all *burger-flipping* service-sector jobs that are prevalent in food service, retail sales, and cleaning and maintenance. Add to these various forms of warehouse, car-hailing and delivery type jobs, most of which pay close to the minimum wage with few benefits, and the picture takes on a gloomy hue. By the way, as many as 30% of the US workforce - over 40 million workers - are employed in the low-end service sector. So, as the middle seems to be hollowing out, many workers appear to be falling through the cracks into jobs that barely pay living wages.

Recently, what could be described as a double whammy has begun to erode many middle-class jobs that were presumed to be safe. Workers at risk include insurance underwriters, bill collectors, travel agents, executive secretaries, office number-crunchers, desktop publishers, reporters and correspondents, to name a few. Surveys show that over 40% of US jobs are highly susceptible to partial or full automation. Furthermore, the maturing of robotics technology and artificial intelligence indicate that most rules-based business processes can be disrupted. Hence, white-collar vocations performed by paralegals, bookkeepers, statisticians, and such are now under serious threat.

Safe Haven?

Historically, past predictions of mass unemployment due to technological change mercifully proved to be inaccurate. We should hope that new, yet unimaginable, jobs will be created in the future to replace those that are disappearing. However, there is no guarantee.

Having said that, as the baby-boom generation comes of age, and the world's population becomes greyer in the coming decades, occupations that seem to be enjoying a big boost are nursing and social-assistance jobs. In fact, demand for home healthcare workers, who should be better appreciated and paid more, is projected to grow markedly. Even though the education sector is being reinvented while undergoing disruption by communications technology, teachers will continue to provide invaluable service to future generations of students.

More broadly, jobs that depend on a high degree of dexterity, creativity and social intelligence may be shielded from the relentless onslaught of high technology, at least for the foreseeable future.

On the political front, democratic governments must recognise that the path to legitimacy and social harmony lies in reducing economic inequality, and one way to achieve this objective is by strengthening and securing the middle class.

Post-Coronavirus Outbreak

If the news from China is accurate, the Chinese may have turned the corner on the coronavirus crisis. While the country still faces the risk of a second wave, and must cope with the challenge of policing its borders from external infection, the Chinese state is rushing to revive its economy. Despite their best efforts, economic growth in China has already taken a big hit this year.

The American economy, the world's largest, has its work cut out before it recovers from the economic damage inflicted by the pandemic. The number of workers filing claims for unemployment benefits, including those who have been laid off or are under furlough, has reached unprecedented levels. Like other nations who have attempted to bolster their economies by passing stimulus legislation, economic activity has nevertheless hit a brick wall in most industries, most glaringly the airline industry.

When normalcy finally returns, no one is certain how many jobs would have survived nor the scope of structural changes that would have occurred. Possibly, lingering uncertainty may prove to be as elusive an enemy as the coronavirus. And for employers and employees alike, these are indeed distressing times.

The suggestion may seem preposterous and counter-intuitive in the extreme. Nevertheless, is it possible that the employment crisis being wrought by automation and digital technology could, in the end, be remedied by the same drivers? Hopefully, brand new and dignified middle-class jobs might emerge in forms that will surprise and delight the most ardent doomsayers.

CHAPTER 38

Lucrative Side Hustles

The 2019 Hollywood movie, *The Hustle*, was premised on the misadventure of two women reputed for swindling gullible old men out of their possessions. Not much of a film plot but, whether in a world of fantasy or the real one, the word *hustle* often connotes disreputable behaviour.

In business parlance, a *side hustle* is a job undertaken in parallel with formal paid employment in order to earn supplemental income. To an old-fashioned employer, a *side job* could be viewed as a surreptitious attempt by an employee to serve two masters, and one can only imagine how well that usually works out. At the extreme, there are people who take on part-time jobs with a second employer after closing hours. Out of necessity, some might even clock time over the weekend, but such indefatigable hustlers are few and far between.

More commonly, there are employees who genuinely loathe their day job, and who seek escape in a fun pastime or hobby that just happens to bring in extra income.

True Passion

For workers whose passion for their *side job or side gig* exceeds their commitment to their regular job, which may not bode well for their career prospects. Also, if the earnings from the former exceeds the wages realized from the latter, that could represent a tipping point when a stark decision has to be made. A recurring challenge would be how to navigate the conflicts of interest that often ensue.

In other words, if the *side job* becomes sufficiently lucrative with a promising future, it could precipitate permanent time out on formal employment. But we may be getting ahead of ourselves. Perhaps we should backtrack by first reviewing the nature of hobbies, assess the characteristics of a dual work lifestyle, and explore the range of *side gigs* that are out there.

Hobbies

If a hobby is an activity we pursue in our spare time primarily for pleasure, then it could presumed to be voluntary. Most day jobs are the exact opposite, which typically are undertaken to put food on the table. By that logic, any hobby that yields monetary value is a blessing in disguise. Furthermore, if that same idea grows into a bona fide business, then the entrepreneurial spirit can be presumed to be alive and well in that individual.

Traditionally, leisure activities such as photography, cooking, sewing, woodcarving, and such creative tinkering could be classified as hobbies. People with the discipline to structure and organise a hobby into a project, with a defined beginning and end, are usually best positioned to succeed as home-based entrepreneurs.

With the passage of time, starting with the millennial generation, the ubiquity of digital technology has expanded beyond our wildest imagination the frontier and variety of creative pursuits. Notwithstanding, the challenge will always be how to translate a hobby into a viable product or service. A good first step is to conduct market research and analysis. Doing so will help to define your market, identify potential customers, where they are located, and whether you can actually fulfil market demand.

Next, you should conduct a pilot run by testing your business idea on a handful of customers, fine-tune your product or service, obtain customer feedback, and monitor your cash flow. If everything stacks up, you may be ready to convert your hobby into a *side hustle*, which may entail licensing, registrations, building a website, and creating a marketing strategy.

Dual Work Lifestyle

So, for people engaged in a standard 9-to-5 job while juggling a *side gig*, how exactly do they balance such a dual work lifestyle? Let us agree that it is a very bad idea for anyone to cheat their employer during a normal workday by secretly indulging in semi-clandestine activities. Not only is it unethical, but by undercutting one's employer and under-performing on the job, such a practice could well result in the eventual loss of that job.

Ideally, some hobbies are best left to weekends or idle times. However, if it is an activity conducted virtually or online, then time, distance and place may no longer be insurmountable barriers. In that event, putting in an extra hour or two before bedtime or snatching odd moments outside of normal working hours has now become commonplace.

Watch Your Costs

Having identified and settled on a *side hustle* that makes money, the road to sustainability can often be traced to the ability to manage costs. While it would be expected that a new business will require some initial investment, a break-even point ought not to be too far over the horizon otherwise the venture could turn into a sinking hole.

The practice of bookkeeping, by accounting properly for revenue and costs, can now be achieved using one of several software applications that are available online. The benefits of inculcating good business practices early on cannot be over-emphasized, well before a *side hustle* grows into a full-fledged business venture.

Traditional Ventures

For those who may have a learnt a trade, had exposure to vocational training, or picked up useful technical and functional skills in their youth, several opportunities to leverage such aptitudes into *side hustles* exist. Take cooking for example, anyone who loves food and enjoys entertaining others can choose to become a personal chef or caterer, outside of their regular job.

Those who are proficient in one musical instrument or another can leverage such skills by offering musical lessons. Although it is difficult to scale up such a venture, since a teacher can only deliver a fixed number of lessons, nevertheless the hours are predictable and hardly any investment is required. For women, there is always demand for babysitting or nanny services, which is a relatively easy way of earning extra cash.

Other practical *side jobs* include providing driving lessons, fitness training, offering interior decorating services, and doing odd jobs in the neighbourhood. In the West, for those who love animals, there is money to be made by walking dogs or providing pet grooming services. Relatively speaking, these could be classified as easy *side jobs* compared to those that are intellectually more challenging.

Since the 1990s, when the World Wide Web took off, the interesting fact is that there is hardly any business enterprise, however insignificant, that does not find it useful to set up a website. The majority of such websites are basic, information-only sites that, at the minimum, provide *About Us*, *Services* and *Contact Us* particulars.

As the Internet matured, the impact of information technology on bricks-and-mortar industries rose steadily from the turn of the new millennium onwards. Computer scientists and coders became more prominent in the economy as the demand for software developers grew. The arrival of mobile devices and mobile apps would continue the trend. Even today, anyone with coding skills can, in their spare time, dabble in website and app development, all of which have ushered in what we now refer to as the gig economy.

The Gig Economy

In contrast with a traditional 9-to-5 job, gig workers are remunerated on the basis of the number of individual "*gigs*" they undertake. *Gigs* are usually freelance or short-term contracts which, by their nature, are highly flexible in terms of working hours and conditions.

The most stereotypical *gigs* involve ride-hailing and parcel- or food-delivery services for easily accessible *cash jobs*. They offer the employer, such as *Uber*, *Lyft* and *PostMates*, a lot of flexibility and the worker much independence, but little or nothing in terms of health insurance and employee benefits.

In terms of independence and flexibility, the Internet has provided those referred to as freelancers and teleworkers diverse opportunities to market their skill sets across the globe. Sites like *Flexjobs, Upwork* and *Fiverr* are three of the most popular in this genre. They offer lucrative *on-demand gigs* such as resume writing, proofreading and translation services, for those who can deliver value at the right price point.

For anyone with graphic design skills, a site like *99Designs* can help to launch exceptional talents by showcasing their work to prospective clients. Brand management is a related field that designers can tap into as a *side job* from home. EBooks and audio books have gained in popularity, which provide a tremendous opportunity for those with good writing skills to earn money on the side. *Skype* offers online tutors an avenue to impart knowledge interactively, while *YouTube* is the go-to channel for packaged tutorials, both of which can engender *side income*.

All told, platforms such as *eBay*, *Craigslist*, *YouTube*, *Etsy*, *CafePress*, *ClickFunnels*, and numerous others provide innumerable latitude for anyone with the drive, passion and imagination to pioneer new *side hustle* schemes or to take full advantage of existing ideas that have spawned some of the best *side jobs* around.

The Future...

Although no one can predict the future, the unfortunate but all too real coronavirus outbreak promises to reshape the global economy in ways that we can only speculate about.

Based on early signs, it seems that many conventional jobs could be lost and may not return at the end of this crisis. It is also certain that *side gigs* are here to stay, and may well propagate on new marketplaces where pro-active entrepreneurs will be able to supplement their income.

www.ingramcontent.com/pod-product-compliance
Lightning Source LLC
Chambersburg PA
CBHW072027230526
45466CB00020B/1040